Contracts in Plain English

RICHARD WINCOR

Contracts in Plain English

New York
St. Louis
San Francisco
Auckland
Düsseldorf
Johannesburg
Kuala Lumpur
London
Mexico
Montreal
New Delhi
Panama
Paris
São Paulo

McGRAW-HILL BOOK COMPANY

Singapore
Sydney
Tokyo
Toronto

Library of Congress Cataloging in Publication Data

Wincor, Richard.
Contracts in plain English.

Includes index.
1. Legal composition. 2. Contracts. I. Title.
Law 808'.066'34602021 75-20252
ISBN 0-07-070966-1

1234567890 BPBP 732109876

The editors for this book were W. Hodson Mogan and Beatrice Carson, the designer was Naomi Auerbach, and the production supervisor was Teresa F. Leaden. It was set in Palatino by University Graphics, Inc.

Printed and bound by The Book Press.

For Daisy

Contents

Preface

The uses of English are well documented. There are books about Middle English, Jane Austen's English, the East Anglian dialect, Australian idioms, medical jargon, and Flemish loanwords, enough to afford occupation for life to the keenest scholar. Still, the portrait is incomplete. A figure is missing from this varied and rich canvas.

The missing figure is somebody doing business in Japan, or the Netherlands, or Wyoming. Doing business means working out agreements with other people, sometimes elaborate contracts bristling with "Whereas" clauses and sometimes nothing but little standard forms, exchanges of letters, conversations at lunch that share one unifying characteristic, a habit of turning the golden language of Shakespeare and Dickens into a minefield.

Nowadays more and more agreements are made in English. German is useful in Eastern Europe, Spanish in larger areas, but English is the nearest thing we have to a universal business language. Joint ventures, bank loans, and trademark licenses frequently are spelled out in this language even though it is not native to at least one of the contracting parties. There lies the danger; all too often the people involved go wrong and pay heavily for it. No captain of industry takes out his own appendix, but somehow wording a contract seems less risky.

And so we have identified the missing figure. It can be anyone: a Japanese buying television rights in London or an American ordering machinery from the Germans. Ideally each of them will have a lawyer at hand reviewing every communication that goes out or comes in. But for those who go part of the way to contract without legal advice, and perhaps too for international lawyers in countries where English is an auxiliary language, this book may be helpful in avoiding the worst pitfalls. Contract language can be the instrument of order, clarity, even a touch of style. All too often, however, it explodes in the hand.

What are some of the dangers? At least five tend to recur in gloomy pattern, filling up casebooks with a Legal Theater of the Absurd played by unwilling actors. They are:

1. Contracts never intended to be contracts
2. Agreements that fail as contracts where the opposite was intended
3. Contracts so unclear as to be interpreted contrary to what one side intended
4. Contracts neglecting to cover one or more of the main points
5. Contracts impossible of performance because of external impediments such as exchange control regulations

Any one of these can put a company out of business. Nevertheless one finds Germans, Czechs, whoever can just about order dinner in English, making commitments by letter or telex in language that may be fatal to their enterprises. Many whose native language is English are only a little less reckless. With the stakes so high, it would be better to forgo bravery and pursue caution.

This is not a lawbook, and its treatment of contract law is intended only to bring out the impact of certain words and phrases under one of the main legal systems of the world. That system is the common law, now much amended by statute everywhere, which developed in England and soon flourished in many parts of the world. Here and there remnants of Roman law and other systems remain side by side with the English concepts—in Scotland and Louisiana, for example—while in Europe the common law never took root at all, and in

Asia some of it mingled with local doctrines and produced hybrids. In this book only common law contract principles are cited. Even these can differ radically according to area, but they serve as background for the understanding of specialized language, just as you must know something about medieval astrology to appreciate Chaucer. Perhaps one distinction is justified: that misunderstanding of Chaucer's zodiac will only limit your aesthetic and philosophical experience, while misunderstanding of Contract English can mean bankruptcy.

Accordingly this book sets out some of the main lines of contract law and goes on, after certain reflections on English itself, to consider the two together in extended examples ranging from casual business inquiries to elaborate contracts. No specific advice is offered, and no forms appear. The goal is different: to suggest, implant, nurture, cultivate, rehearse, confirm, review, belabor, and exemplify, until it becomes a reflex, a certain style of thought and expression for dealing in English.

What style can be worthy of such emphasis? The term "Position-taking Style" commends itself as the most descriptive. The Position-taking Style is above all unspontaneous and controlled. It is also courteous, precise, and evasive by turns, wary of commitments but quick in their recognition. It may be thought of as simplified legalese or a low dialect of diplomacy. Its trademark is caution, its raison d'être the potency of words, its usefulness incalculable. The Position-taking Style makes communication into a game of chess.

In the right hands, something equally important, it promotes honor. In this language it will be more difficult to make promises never meant to be kept, easier to hold somebody to his or her word. If good fences make good neighbors, good contracts make good business partners.

The phrase "his or her" leads to another point: there is need for a new contract vocabulary suitable to either gender. The subject is discussed briefly in Chapter 6. In this book the generic "he" is generally used but only for the purpose of succintness, and it is always intended to refer to both women and men.

Contract English is scarcely the best vehicle for dinner conversation or its frequent aftermath. It has its place, worded in the Position-taking Style, wherever business is transacted, serving usefully as a law-shaped industrial jargon tailored always to the accomplishment of a specific outcome. It serves also as a prompter for the inarticulate and a muzzle for the enthusiast.

What happens if you receive a letter saying "I am glad everything is worked out," or even a cable with just the word "Bravo"? A little feeling for Contract English will put you on guard if these phrases follow negotiations which you have decided to bring to an end. Even declining to answer may be taken to mean agreement. Immediate disavowal is the safe course. Similarly, if your proposal to a British firm is replied to by cable saying "Bob's your uncle," it will be unsafe to assume that you have an agreement. That old-fashioned phrase is little known outside England, and even there it means vague things such as "well then," "there it is," actually "voilà," but not clearly "We accept your offer." In that case it would be useful to request clarification.

These few precepts remind us that the great language of blank verse and sonnets has had to go out into the world and earn a living. The same thing happened with Latin and its dialects hundreds of years ago. For better or worse, and whatever we think of it, English is now engaged in trade. In what follows we consider ways of helping it to success.

Acknowledgments are due Cherry Watson for typing the manuscript and Rita Spannagl-Drescher for supplying the text of the multilanguage treaty.

Richard Wincor

Contracts
in
Plain
English

PART ONE

CHAPTER ONE

The Legal Background

Contract law is a complex and vastly documented subject. Only a lawyer can deal with it on a serious level, and only a monk can know all of the published literature that expounds it. A number of basic principles, however, can be outlined sufficiently to mark off encounters that require the use of specialized English. As a beginning we look at the terrain generally.

Three Contract Stages

In the main there are three stages in transactions involving business contracts: first, negotiation of the terms; second, drafting documents reflecting these terms; and all too often, third, litigation to enforce or avoid them or to find out their meaning. Perhaps a fourth might be added, the administration of contracts, where a company keeps orderly track of option dates and other documented points requiring vigilance; however, that becomes a question of choosing the right people, and this book is about choosing the right words.

Of the three stages listed, the third can be ruled out straightaway on the ground that it belongs properly in the lawbooks. Consequently we shall not deal with breach of contract, or the measure of damages, or rescission for fraud, or a variety of other matters that are handed over to lawyers when things go wrong.

Neither shall we consider questions of evidence, although everyone appears nearly as concerned with proof as with the event to be proved. Evidence is another subject for professionals in the courtroom. Let us assume throughout the balance of our discussions that everything can be proved by the sworn testimony of a dozen abbotts and a tape recorder. The best practical advice is to keep copies of all correspondence and memoranda of important discussions.

That leaves two contract stages: negotiation and drafting. The second is also best left to the lawyers, but sometimes this is not done, and even more often the line between negotiation and actually making contract commitments escapes even the responsible executive who intends calling in the lawyer to write formal documents. Formalities, however, are not what make contracts.

We are concerned, then, with negotiations and the wording of all communications up to the formal contract itself. Later on even the formal contract will be put under the microscope, but not until earlier stages of its formation have been examined.

Summing up, and in everyday terms, a typical first stage of contract is two people having a drink and talking about future dealing. A second phase might be letters written back and forth working out points of agreement. The third we have placed out of bounds, since the object of what follows is to prevent disputes.

In these two earlier stages it will be helpful to know something about rules of contract. But whose rules? Different nations borrow or create different legal systems, and even within a single country the rules may vary according to region or status or the kind of transaction involved. Consequently a preliminary question is often what law applies.

Choice of Law

The importance of this point can be illustrated by a single example. Assume that a trademark owner in the Republic of A contracted to assign his trademark to an unrelated company in the United Provinces of B, and for a good price. In A it is quite legal to assign trademarks without selling with them any part of the business they symbolize. In B, however, a contract to assign trademarks this casually is unlawful. In A the mark is considered property that its owner can sell to anyone of his choosing. In B any such cavalier transfer would be considered deceptive; consumers would buy on the strength of a name that no longer meant what they thought it did. Two opposite philosophies collide.

International dealings are not the only collision areas. An Englishman dealing in Scotland or an American dealing in Louisiana may stumble on relics of Roman law. Even a New Yorker making a contract in Massachusetts will have to revise his concepts if the contract is for the benefit of a third party. Similarly an Indonesian in his own country may be subject to native adat law for one thing and to modified Dutch law for another.

Since this book is about English, it will be assumed that English common law systems apply. This assumption is made, however, only for the purpose of analyzing contract language in what follows. It is most emphatically not a safe assumption to make if you are negotiating with people outside the United States, England, Canada, Australia, New Zealand, Singapore, Penang, and Malacca. In some countries the legal history reflects English common law influence, for example in South Africa, where the Roman-Dutch system is supplemented by reference to British cases, or in India, where the Indian Contract Act of 1872 combined English and local concepts. In other countries the common law background is alien. Throughout Western Europe the main concepts were Roman, not English. In nearly all cases so much of the original system has been codified that the distinctions are largely historical, but not entirely so. Different concepts remain, even among nations outside the socialist world, where once again you find different points of view.

But disharmony is not in itself fatal. There is no reason why many contracts cannot get by under the different national and treaty systems that affect them. Contracts in English suggest Anglo-American contract rules, but you can still do a deal with a Dutchman.

The main point is always to be aware that there are differences. How these can be resolved usually is a problem for lawyers. An entire field of study known as Conflict of Laws has been devoted to some of the problems arising out of the clash between legal systems. With contracts the applicable law may be the law of the place where the contract is made; in other cases it may be the law of the place where the contract is to be performed. In preliminary negotiations, however, most business people will find it impractical to master the subject.

What they can do, and very often in fact do, is specify which system of law is to apply. At some point in most international negotiations there will be room for this issue to be worked out. Each side is likely to propose its own law as the more familiar and presumably congenial. A great many considerations, including taxes, will be taken into account in the solution.

Specifying what law is to govern a proposed contract is a practical device. You can go just so far with it if you try importing a foreign system that violates the law where the contract is to be performed. For example, if the Principality of X permitted slavery, you could still not get by with a slavery contract in Leeds or Chicago by stipulating that it was governed by the law of X. Aside from such limitations, however, every negotiator is well advised to keep choice of law in mind. If a sensible choice can be agreed to, then at least the ground rules will be known in advance.

Freedom versus Regulations

Something else to consider besides choice of law is the question of freedom to contract in general. Theoretically the Anglo-Saxon system allows people to agree as they please, as long as the agreement stops short of violating law or public policy. This concept reflects a laissez-faire capitalist approach characteristic of industrialized Western nations. Its popularity is dwindling, and the scope of its applicability shrinks by the hour. Instead, contracts are increasingly subject to regulation everywhere.

A moment's reflection suggests a great many areas in which larger interests restrict freedom of contract. Nearly everywhere there are laws concerning interest rates, zoning, racial and sexual discrimination, exchange control, consumer protection, and other matters that narrow the scope of what can be privately agreed upon. Collective bargaining shapes the conditions of employment in growing measure.

Earlier we considered awareness of different legal systems and the practical value of agreeing on your own choice. Now a second level of awareness deserves cultivation: awareness of impediments on the freedom to make private agreements. Such and such a clause may violate U.S. antitrust law or European Economic Community (EEC) law under the Rome Treaty—choice of law comes into it again—and something else may be void under Czech law or impossible to guarantee in the United Kingdom. Here, as before, nobody is likely to know all of the pitfalls. Once again, awareness is half the battle.

The most practical move is to make your commitments explicitly subject to overcoming various impediments. If you prove unable to surmount them, then your agreement never takes effect, or certain provisions in it never take effect, whichever best suits the occasion. Sometimes the impediment will be named, for example with exchange control permission, where British payment in dollars might be hinged on Bank of England approval. In other instances the intruding regulation or law is impossible of advance identification but serves nevertheless as an escape route with no street name. One example might be making your promise subject to the minimum rules and rates of any union having jurisdiction or to the applicable laws and regulations of Thailand.

And so it now appears that everyone is well advised to look carefully to the left and the right before beginning contract discussions. At the left is an array of foreigners, each with his own idea of the law, and the trick is to find a companion with concepts nearest your own. At the right is a mass of officials representing the public interest, or special interests, and you must somehow make sure that you propose nothing they are likely to overrule.

A quick backward glance may be useful too.

Prior Conflicting Commitments

On this subject little need be said, because it should be obvious that nobody can rightfully commit something which conflicts with a previous contract commitment to somebody else. Nevertheless it happens time and again. One memorable example is a singer agreeing to record exclusively for three different record companies. This individual's good nature is to be applauded, but it does tend to create difficulties.

Perhaps this subject belongs under the heading we have bypassed with only brief mention—contract administration. Somebody in the company ought to keep records and be sure that proposed contracts will not put you in breach of a previous one still in effect. The recording of a song is only one field where people go wrong in this respect. Any business enterprise with multiple commitments has to see to it that they fit together. It takes study and may require making a little chart to be sure none of the undertakings conflict, but it will be well worth doing.

When you come to making formal agreements, the other side is likely to require warranties that no previous contracts or other impediments stand in the way of your new obligations. Even without formal warranties the same thing may be implied, so that sooner or later you come face to face with the need to avoid violating prior conflicting commitments. Sooner is better.

Capacity to Contract

Looking straight ahead at last, we find the contract adversary, the person with whom we are dealing, which raises an altogether new point worth mentioning. Can the other side make good its promises? The question here is less one of intent than of legal capacity. Once again an outlandish example hammers home the point.

Somebody called to a meeting might be taken aback if his opposite number turned out to be twelve years old. Similarly the tea girl might undertake major commitments on behalf of her corporate employer (as distinct from individual commitments) only to be disavowed by the company after papers were drawn. Obviously neither of these persons had the power to bind, and in the case of the infant this want of capacity would almost surely apply to himself as well as to the company for whom he purported to act as spokesman.

These examples are not at all perplexing, even if a little whimsical, but problems of this kind bedevil major industries and cause damage. All you need do is substitute president for the child or managing director for the tea girl to see how it actually happens. Frequently a high-up official or agent gives reason to believe that he speaks definitively for his company. At the last minute a cable arrives announcing regrets, but "The Board" refuses to go along. A sense of betrayal follows, and sometimes a lawsuit.

The corporation itself may be incapable of delivering on its promise if the promise exceeds its charter powers. Again the wrong corporate entity may be used, a subsidiary for example, against which there is no useful recourse for breach of contract. One who begins hearing that "our foreign partnership takes the contract for tax reasons" had better start asking questions.

Asking questions is the practical way to begin dealing with these problems. In the most polite way you can try and pin down how far your opposite number can go in making commitments. What is his or her position? Is everything subject to somebody else's approval? Is the right corporate entity negotiating by its authorized deputy? Is its plan at the last minute to assign everything to a tax shelter company in a locale with palm trees? In brief, can the people you deal with make good what they say?

Asking questions is just the beginning. Later on it will be helpful to have confirmation in writing and on proper company letterheads. The company may still disavow and say that their representative was unauthorized, but that raises questions concerning agency and makes betrayal a little bit more difficult.

The opposite side of the coin is our own power to make commitments. All of the same question are worth asking about ourselves as we get in deeper and deeper. The right thing is always to draw clear lines between what we can deliver and what needs approval by others. So modest an approach is unhelpful for ego but to be recommended nonetheless for its other qualities.

A Brief Review

At this stage it will be useful to review the reasons for looking in all four directions before you begin making contracts.

First, there will often be the question of what legal system applies, and while this chapter is about English common law principles, the Germans and Czechs may not have read it. One must be aware of the point and may be able to specify that the law of a particular place will govern the contract.

Second, certain promises and entire contracts, for that matter, may be impossible to perform unless the state or other authority grants permission to do so. Again awareness is half the way to solution, and the rest lies in making promises conditional on the happening of the desired event, such as official clearance.

Third, anyone with a business history is likely to have earlier contracts still in effect. As a matter of routine it will be helpful to make sure that they create no conflict with proposed new agreements.

Fourth, dealing with different companies and ranks raises the question of capacity to make binding commitments. Whether the other side has the capacity to keep promises, and whether its representatives are authorized to make them, should be explored delicately at the beginning and pinned down less and less delicately as discussions proceed.

Even these preliminary steps are best taken with legal advice. This outline confirms the need for it.

Fundamentals of Contract

At this point we put aside preliminary inquiries and come to grips more directly with English as an international contract language. According to plan we deal first with the legal background, so that later the selection of particular words and phrases can be made to suit the desired purpose. The system to be treated is common law as it relates to contracts. Its exposition is much oversimplified and designed only as background to a style of English, not as the solution to legal problems. That it may help avoid them, however, is not beyond possibility, and to suggest habits of thought has its practical uses. One of the most practical is in shaping expression.

Assume now that all four preliminary steps have been taken. Our contractor-to-be has looked East and West, North and South, as recommended, doing whatever can be done in the earliest stages. Everyone agrees that the law of New York applies, for example. Payment in dollars is clearly subject to Bank of England approval, with alternatives agreed to. The company historian has burrowed in the stacks for a week without finding any conflicting contracts that get in the way of proposed arrangements. The main spokeswoman for the other side is Board Chairman and shows a certified resolution authorizing what she proposes to do on behalf of an honorable and solvent company. So far, everything is in order. Now the question arises, what is a contract? Putting it a little differently, when is there a binding commitment? How is it formed, and by what characteristics can it be recognized?

There are three basic elements of any contract: offer, acceptance, and consideration. At least this is the case where Anglo-Saxon traditions have shaped contract law. Consequently a brief glance at each, and at some of their companion doctrines, is in order.

Offer An offer may be considered a promise conditioned on a return promise of performance or on an act by the other side. For our purposes it may be recognized by a proposal of definite terms, communicated to another party, whose acceptance in circumstances where mutual assent to these terms is manifested may result in a contract. An offer must be distinguished from an invitation to negotiate, but even if sufficiently definite to escape this lesser status it may still be withdrawn before the recipient accepts it, with the result that no contract ensues. The offering party may, however, stipulate time limits and even specific modes for acceptance as a condition of contract.

Offers are usually the subject of several complex chapters in law treatises, and extended analysis would be out of place in a book mainly about English. A few examples should be more to the point than a discussion of legal theory.

Shimizu in Tokyo begins thinking about building an electronics plant in the Netherlands. He writes up an elaborate proposal and buries it in his desk. Since nothing has been communicated and there is nothing to accept, no offer was made.

Shimizu writes to Van Scheltinga that "we might be interested in building a plant near Leiden using your facilities and would welcome your views with a schedule of price estimates." Nothing definite, no offer, only an invitation to begin talking.

But if Tokyo issues an elaborate and detailed proposal setting out all of the material points, that may constitute an offer if susceptible of acceptance by return promises or acts parallel to what was offered. Phrases such as "price and other terms to be negotiated" probably are too vague to support offers, but if Shimizu gets close enough to the bone by dealing with all the important conditions he will be considered to have made a firm offer, which the Dutch side can take up by communicating acceptance. How this is done is considered next.

Acceptance It was mentioned earlier that mutual assent must be manifested before the offer ripens into contract. Now we look at things from the Dutch side.

If Van Scheltinga likes the proposal but dawdles and says nothing, he may lose out because the offer expires either within its own recited time limit or within a reasonable time if there was no fixed limit in the proposed terms. On the other hand his silence cannot be considered acceptance; otherwise people would be always threatened with having a bone thrust down the throat with letters such as "If we do not hear from you by Friday we shall consider that you have accepted our offer and that a contract exists." That kind of thing would be intolerable.

Aside from time limits, the manner of acceptance may be vital. A whimsical offer stipulating that acceptance must be communicated by carrier pigeon cannot, unless there are special circumstances, be taken up by cable.

Thus far we have considered acceptance by the communication of promises or counterpromises. What may be a little more difficult to envision is acceptance by acts, by doing something that manifests assent to the terms offered. Nevertheless this is a favorite in lawbooks although rather less likely to happen in serious industry. If the offer invites shipment of certain articles under fixed terms, and the shipments are made, it seems probable that the offer has been accepted. That would be one example; the more usual one has a landowner telling the neighbor's child, "I will give you five dollars for mowing my lawn," which the youngster accepts by mowing the lawn even though maintaining a sullen silence throughout this exercise.

Since we are concerned with industry rather than housekeeping, it will be useful to show where acceptance usually goes wrong at a serious level. Time and again you will find variations on the following theme.

Shimizu transmits a detailed offer to Van Scheltinga, who replies somewhat in this fashion: "Thank you for the detailed and fair proposal in your letter of ———— . We are pleased that negotiations have finally resulted in agreement, and we accept your offer except for two points. In clause 3 of your letter you stipulate completion of Phase One by the end of this year, but this was never discussed and we need at least an additional six months. Similarly at the end you talk about present cost structures, but I made it clear earlier that these change, and we will both have to go along with prices as they may rise in the future in accordance with our company policy. Everything else is correct and we can open the champagne." So they can, but only for refreshment, because there was a counteroffer rather than acceptance. Perhaps minor points could be overlooked, but time limits and prices go to the essence.

What must Shimizu do in these circumstances? Theoretically he need do nothing. His offer has been rejected, and his silence, as we saw earlier, is no acceptance of the counterproposal. As a practical matter, however, he risks litigation by silence and is better advised to cable or write immediately that there is no contract. Whether he revives his original offer, with or without time limits, is determined by business considerations.

From the opposite point of view it may be that the Dutch company needs the Japanese contract to stay in business. In that case Van Scheltinga studies every communication from Tokyo with great care for an appropriate opportunity to reply, "We accept." Some of the terms may be disappointing, but on balance the contract is salvation. Acceptance is unconditional and in the required manner. In this case any last-minute quibbling may be fatal.

The point is that nobody can pick and choose the terms he likes in an offer and reject the others. Putting it a little differently, picking and choosing is a luxury to be indulged only if you can afford the risk of losing a contract. The point seems obvious but escapes many.

Consideration Even if an offer is properly accepted you need a third element before a contract exists. This third element is called "consideration" and is highly unpopular and likely to become more so as different legal systems affect one another. Nevertheless it constitutes a necessary ingredient in contracts governed by classic Anglo-Saxon legal principles.

Consideration is an element of bargain, a quid pro quo, doing or forbearing to do something you were not previously bound to do or avoid doing except for the contract. Some writers deal with it as a detriment to the one making the promise.

For example, a letter saying "We admire your industrial policies at the Leeds factory and should like to contribute £10,000 as a gesture of solidarity" gets the Leeds people nowhere even if they unequivocally "accept." Leeds incurs no detriment, offers nothing in exchange unless there is an implied promise to continue the same policies, so the contract fails for want of consideration. All you have is an unenforceable promise.

Next we consider an exchange which appears a valid bargain but is really no better than the other. Somebody writes, "I will stop infringing your trademarks if you pay me $25,000," and the victim accepts. Still there is no consideration; whoever made this offer had no right to infringe trademarks and consequently offered nothing in exchange and gave up nothing for the $25,000.

Here a distinction must be made between settling a legitimate dispute and promising to leave off doing what you had no right to do in the first place. If there were a genuine question as to whether the trademarks were being infringed, then the offer to stop using them would give up something in return for payment. Various settlements of disputes, sometimes called accord and satisfaction, have the necessary ingredient of consideration. Courts may go very far looking for it, but if there is no bargain at all, if the trademark user clearly infringes, then that individual offers nothing in the way of bargain and no contract exists.

Consideration does not have to be any sort of massive detriment making for an equal bargain. The slightest thing may suffice, which is why you often see the phrase "For One Dollar and other valuable consideration" or its equivalent. But there must be something, as distinct from nothing at all, even if you have to go looking under the rug for it. Purely one-sided promises are unlikely to become contracts. A sausage for a yacht, however, is a valid bargain.

Then what is a contract? No single definition suffices, because there are too many exceptions. You may have all of the prime ingredients but still no contract because the promises were induced by fraud or duress. For that reason we avoid any caption entitled "Definition of Contract"; it seems better to mention some of its chief characteristics, just as describing an elephant is less foolhardy than defining one. Nevertheless the features thus far described form a pattern.

A contract in one sense is an actionable promise, that is to say, an agreement which the law will enforce or for whose breach it will afford a remedy. It consists of a bargain and comes into existence when an offer is accepted by a promise or by performance of what was bargained for, and each side limits its otherwise lawful freedom of behavior at least in some nominal degree known as consideration. In commercial terms a contract is a binding commitment.

Reliance What happens if someone relies on a promise without all the trappings of offer, acceptance, and consideration? Conceivably it may prove expensive, and, if his reliance was reasonable, it would be unfair to leave him with no recourse against broken promises.

Certain commitments made under seal are enforced without the need for consideration, but in commercial negotiations we are concerned more with informal communication than with antique practices. The law does, in some circumstances, support promises that stand outside the rigid structure outlined earlier.

Reliance is the key notion here. Two examples in this very complex area suggest what you must look out for. In proposing them we forgo once again any discussion of legal theory and instead show you how to recognize the alarm signal in practice.

In the first example a promise to reduce a tenant's rent is made without formalistic consideration. The tenant relies on it, perhaps giving up an opportunity of taking different space at a lower figure. The landlord may be denied the original higher rent on these facts under a doctrine known as promissory estoppel.

The second example concerns third parties outside the original dealings between the two who are making a contract. If Shimizu and Van Scheltinga agree that a distributor in New York is to have exclusivity for the United States and send him copies of the agreement without contracting with him direct, the American may have reason to rely on these commitments even to the extent of undertaking development expenses. In some cases he will be considered to have enforceable promises even though they run to him indirectly at best. When this happens, the law calls him a third party beneficiary. In England and Massachusetts the law developed without recognition of this bizarre status, but elsewhere it turns up as another escape from formalism.

If you lead somebody into relying on promises, it may not always be easy to disavow on the ground that there was no consideration running direct to the proposed beneficiary. Reliance is another alarm signal. If it can be considered reasonable and someone changes position as the result of it, there may be a binding commitment.

Form By now it will be clear that no particular form introduced by "Whereas" clauses is necessary in making contracts. Three further examples expand the point.

In the first, two people work out an entire agreement orally. Offer, consideration, and acceptance are all present with no hedging and nothing important left out. There is just one thing: nobody has written anything down. Certain purely oral agreements, however, can be enforced. The rules vary according to locale, but if the contract is to be performed within a year, and is not an agreement relating to land, it may stand up without written documentation. Especially in this age of recording devices the unwritten contract looms everywhere. If it meets the tests outlined earlier there may be little comfort in arguing that it never was reduced to writing. The moral is best expressed by a World War II slogan: "Loose lips sink ships."

The second example of informality triumphant is the outside reference. In many instances a contract refers to some document or to another agreement which exists elsewhere. If the latter varies from or contradicts the written contract which purports to set out the complete agreement between the people involved, it will be inadmissable under what is called the parol evidence rule. Notes of previous negotiations, however, may be allowed in court where the contract is sufficiently unclear, and they will be worth keeping on file. Considerably more useful as a practical device is something known as incorporation by reference. Here the parties to a contract stipulate that part of it will be governed by outside rules known to both of them, copies of which are sometimes annexed. They might incorporate agreed rules for the arbitration of disputes, or union collective bargaining agreements, or the rules of the Penang Cocoa Exchange for that matter. Incorporation by reference can save time and conduce to clarity if both sides agree.

The third example illustrative of the point that substance and not form is what counts is the implied promise. Not every contract recites, "We explicitly agree to the following." There are times when binding promises can be reasonably implied. An exclusive agency may exist even though the agent fails explicitly to say that he will perform his function. That promise may be implied by his conduct or in the contract considered in its entirety.

Form, then, is very often insignificant. Informality is commendable as long as it never becomes inaccuracy.

Waivers

Another concept worth knowing about is the waiver. Stripped of legal refinement, this is the abandonment of an advantageous position such as being owed money or having the better hold on a contested franchise. If you intend deliberately to yield the edge, so be it; but waivers are frequently blundered into as the result of imprecise language reflecting imprecise thought. Whether or not they require the support of consideration to become effective varies according to the facts and local statutes. The question here is whether or not they are intended, as a matter of business policy.

An example of a waiver might be a letter written in flaming anger to a distributor selling in unauthorized territories. One might be tempted to write something like "You have damaged us and we are going to sue you for a cool million." Aside from the dated quality of its prose, reflecting as it does the viewing of too many old films on television, the quoted phrase may unintentionally be giving something away, namely the right to stop the distributor by injunction, which is rather different from winning damages for his previous wrongdoing. Giving things away is unusual in a business situation; the practice is generally more appropriate for weddings and Christmas.

For this reason you may often find expressions such as "without prejudice" and "not intended as a waiver" in letters and other documents. They sound rude but are frequently worth using, unless the writer is certain of not giving anything away in a disputed position or is so benevolently disposed as to celebrate Yuletide the year round.

Thus far we have considered mainly the ways of getting into and keeping out of or giving up binding commitments. Once commitments are undertaken, however, various patterns recur that shape their dimensions. Later on we shall examine some of these in Contract English, but at this early stage it may be useful to mention four favorites.

Options

The first is known as an option. This popular device is simply a hedged bet, the right to make up your mind about something later on, with the subject matter of your uncertainty immobilized on the shelf until the time limit specified for decision. Options are mainly for saving money. A commitment to buy stock shares costs X; but if a small down payment holds the right to do so in reserve, with payment completed only if the option is exercised, the option holder is better fixed and can back off with honor if events make it advisable.

The escape clause is the option's companion piece. It creates a right to have second thoughts and get out before going the whole way in performing an obligation. Often the two concepts amount pretty much to the same thing, only with different wording. The option in essence means, "We have until May to decide and signify on written notice whether we choose to go ahead with this and pay the balance." The escape clause sounds more go-ahead but suddenly doubles back: "We will pay so and so for the year but can change our minds and get out of it by notifying you no later than May 1 of our decision." Either way, presumably, some small payment is made at the beginning for the right to decide later. This initial payment usually is nonreturnable, and so it ought to be. The phrase "buying time" suggests that it has its price.

Warranties

A second well-known pattern is the warranty or representation. One party to a contract reassures or promises the other that various things are in fact true. If events prove him false, he "indemnifies" the other and pays for the damages resulting from the misrepresentation. Or, in some cases, the buyer may wish to cancel the contract and recover whatever money or rights have been transferred to the other side.

Suppose somebody in a pub offered to sell Big Ben to a Texan. Surely it would be little enough to expect warranties of ownership in the contract; but the absurdity of the example suggests a practical point which comes up time and again. All the warranties in the world are no use against a penniless liar with no insurance. Sometimes you need more, such as a review of the alleged owner's documents proving title. Once you have examined them, however, should the warranties still hold or are you now on your own to interpret their adequacy and meaning? Theoretically, at least, you may now be in just as good a position as your seller to know what his rights are.

Resolutions of this point vary. Sometimes it will be better to avoid learning too much and to rely instead on what a solvent adversary tells you is true if he backs it with appropriate guarantees. In other circumstances you will want to see for yourself. All this is from the buyer's viewpoint; if you happen to be selling, or granting rights, you will want to confine your warranties or representations and throw as much of the burden as possible on the other side, buying insurance for additional comfort.

Assignability

Professionals dislike leaving it up to the courts to decide whether a contract can be assigned and to whom. Mobility in this respect, even if only to move rights from one corporation to an affiliate for tax reasons, is too important to leave up in the air. Consequently one sees clauses in various documents explicitly granting the right to assign. These usually are circumscribed; you can assign only to subsidiaries, or to named people, or your rights but not obligations.

Once again an outlandish example brings home the point. A charity commissions the best chef and the top dress designer in Paris to furnish their skills in connection with a fund-raising ball. Both find themselves overly committed at the last minute and "assign" their contract commissions to substitutes. Obviously neither is keeping to the bargain, which called for unique skills.

Neither artiste would be likely to get away with it, unless a contract spelled out that it could be done. When you order pheasant you will not want tripe, and when you do business with Pickwick you will not want Micawber.

Fiduciaries

A final pattern worth preliminary mention is the creation of special relationships by contract. Lawyers and doctors acting professionally are rightfully burdened with special standards of behavior without all of it being spelled out in documents. Circumstance, however, may impose similar standards on others, for example the obligation to keep secrets or to account for or disclose dealings with third parties. Contracts of employment often become very specific with reference to certain of these points. Contracts with agents are less frequently characterized by recitations about the keeping of confidence and related duties; the creation of agency supplies it.

In the main one can distinguish between transactions at arm's length and transactions in which A acts on behalf of B or learns secrets from B. In the special categories something more than ethical behavior is required.

Accordingly great care must be taken in characterizing relationships. A preliminary letter saying "I am to be your agent" or something flowery such as "the property remains my sacred trust" may be taken literally, or rather, legally, creating obligations more specialized than what was originally intended. Looking at it from the other side, it may be useful to recite your understanding of fiduciary obligations undertaken by others, when applicable, and to call them by the right name. The expectation of transcendent fidelity calls for proper wording.

Unlawful Statements

A point not directly concerned with contract, but important mainly for preliminary correspondence, is the avoidance of libel, violation of the right of privacy, copyright infringement, and breach of confidence. These subjects require extended treatment in lawbooks, but one example should suffice as a warning.

It is risky to put something of this kind into a business letter: "We have sacked our branch manager in Nairobi, not only because of his professional incompetence and drinking problem but also because he has been robbing us blind. Nevertheless you are free to publish his research notes on wildlife which we found in his desk, even though they are unconnected with company business."

The quoted passage, which it is not essential to memorize, may constitute libel and copyright infringement at the same time. Saying things about people and using their literary property can be hazardous.

And with this protracted aside out of the way, let us return to the more diplomatic language of contracts.

Selected Alarm Words

The principles of contract law outlined in this chapter are united by this common theme: that certain words and phrases reflect or create legal consequences and ought to put everybody on guard when they appear. For convenience they will be referred to as Alarm Words, meaning that the listener or reader encountering them should go on the alert, almost by reflex. In many cases he will take legal counsel. Short of that useful step, he will know at least that something is going on and that his reply requires great care.

Without repeating the reasons, which will be apparent from what has been said earlier, let us list samplings of Alarm Words in differing circumstances.

Our first list sounds the alert when you do not want to be considered bound by contractual obligations. In these negative cases, be on guard when you receive communications containing the following words and phrases:

As agreed
We accept
Reflecting our understanding
According to our deal
Considering your offer
Now that everything is worked out
No remaining points
Unconditional
No further problems
Our laws
Assume you were fully authorized
We have done everything you requested
In consideration of
Relying on
For the benefit of
Annexed
Your obligations
Without prejudice
We consider that you have waived
At our option
Your warranties
And our assignees
Special relationship
Duties
Confidential

There are hundreds of others, but this sampling should suffice. Carrying the argument too far, the phrase "Thank you" might be an

Alarm Phrase because it suggests agreement—"Thank you for what?" occurs to the paranoid. Nevertheless our list fixes a climate for caution.

The next list suggests trouble in the opposite circumstances when you do in fact want very much to have the other side contractually bound:

Subject to
If
Only in the event that
Provided
Open points
Remaining areas
Our discussions
Still waiting for
My colleagues in the company
Board approval
Send to our lawyers
At our option
Another meeting
Preliminary
It looks encouraging

And so on. In some cases a phrase can appear on both lists, for example "at our option," which to the negotiator wanting to be uncommitted suggests that something at least was agreed upon sufficiently to create an option, while someone seeking mutual commitments will find this one insufficient because too much perhaps is left up to the other side. In other cases the Alarm Words are harmless or correctly reflect the position and merit no challenge. Still, there is a vast difference between phrases such as "our agreement" and "our discussions." The first points to a contract, the second to no contract, no meeting of the minds, "we are still talking."

Alarm Words embody alarming thoughts. You may usefully spend a little time composing your own list based on the principles of contract law. More useful still, and certainly more creative, is the development of a style designed for coping with contract hazards and reducing the number of unhappy endings. A style of this kind ought to combine courtesy with a sharp cutting edge, so as to rebut, pounce, and keep the talks going, all at the same time. Most important of all, it must be designed so as to play the game fairly.

The Position-taking Style

Contract English is a script for a reflex assumption of the correct stance. Thus in one scene it directs you to move back, in another forward, taking up disciplined postures one after the other as with morning exercise to keep fit. Posture follows posture, although there never can be set forms, until the student improvises almost by intuition and brings off a series of sound moves in sequence. Even those who are less enthusiastic may fix easier goals and learn at least to stay on their feet.

That these disciplines are verbal, not physical, should encourage anyone who takes little exercise. But how are they accomplished? A little practice in what we call the Position-taking Style is the best training for contract negotiation. First we think out the business objective and its alternatives. Then, opening communication with outsiders, we stay on the alert for Alarm Words and equally for what may be called Opportunity Words, which create opportunities to move in rather than away. Eventually the exchange of communications may ripen into a contract.

Later in this book we consider actual language in the Position-taking Style. In this first chapter, however, we stress concepts rather than words, and so the following example is more notable for position-taking than it is for style.

Imagine that somebody conducting negotiations received a letter containing this sentence: "I told Dr. Wasserkopf about our deal." What would be the correct reply, assuming the quoted sentence to be unwelcome?

Here are two possible answers in the Position-taking Style, one courteous and precise, the second less so:

> 1. "I was surprised to learn from your letter that you have communicated something concerning our negotiations to Dr. Wasserkopf, or to anyone for that matter, and that you told him we had a 'deal.' I must remind you that no contract exists between us, although I hope that we may continue negotiations to the end of resolving the many open points. It would be a good idea if you were to put Wasserkopf straight in this matter."

The second possible reply is less elaborate.

2. "What deal?"

One can go on and on, but some of the alternatives that suggest themselves can be dangerous. Here is one example:

3. "Who is Wasserkopf?"

The trouble with number 3 is that it fails to deny that a contract exists, implying on the contrary that the writer wants to know who has been told of its existence. Rebuttal instead of the satisfaction of curiosity is called for in this example.

Rather than propound others, where you might aim for the accomplishment of something opposite, and pin somebody to a commitment he had in fact undertaken, let us merely sum up by repeating that concept fashions style.

The Position-taking Style is a specialized language for negotiating contracts. Choosing the right words depends on knowing the right things to worry about; both require self-discipline but engender a special sort of creativity.

In the next chapter we examine English as a language for the Position-taking Style. There we shall go looking beyond contract concepts and consider some words and phrases that embody them. In company with our fictional negotiators, we move from the general to the particular.

As a beginning, we consider briefly the nature of English, its history, and its varied forms.

CHAPTER TWO

English as a Contract Language

In Dickens' *The Pickwick Papers,* XXIV, an Ipswich beadle enters the room to make an arrest. This dialogue ensues:

> "My name's Tupman," said that gentleman.
> "My name's Law," said Mr. Grummer.
> "What?" said Mr. Tupman.
> "Law," replied Mr. Grummer, "law, civil power, and execative; them's my titles; here's my authority. Blank Tupman, blank Pickvick—against the peace of our sufferin Lord the King—statitt in that case made and purwided—and all regular. I apprehend you Pickvick! Tupman—the aforesaid."

This illiterate and demented babble embodies popular notions about legal English. It has to be pompous, unclear, and full of words like "aforesaid" to do its job. Never say "before that," for example; "prior thereto" is the right way to say it, or, in legalese, the appropriate expression for same.

English is in fact a latecomer as a legal language. Even after the Norman Conquest court pleadings in England were in French, and before that (or prior thereto) lawyers used Latin. Perhaps some of our difficulties arise because English was unacceptable in its childhood.

English as the subject of this book is the sort of English you would read in a newspaper in New York or London or Brisbane. There would be minor differences between them, but anyone able to read one could understand the others. Their language, however, has a long history and many shapes. The following brief sketch may be helpful.

An Outline of English

Anglo-Saxon, or Old English as it is now called, is arbitrarily dated 500–1100. Old English is incomprehensible without the degree of study required for a foreign language. Highly inflected, as older languages usually are, it sounds like Swedish read by a drug addict. Its literature is rewarding if you like poems about sea monsters and stories about the lives of Christian saints.

Middle English, which brings the reader glimmers of recognition, is considered to have been the language of England from 1100 to 1500. This is the language of Chaucer, when inflections were dying off, but it will be a mistake to suppose that Middle English was all like Chaucer. It was a series of dialects, and Chaucer would have had difficulty with the dialect used by that equal genius, unknown by name, who wrote *Sir Gawain and the Green Knight.* Chaucer's language was London-East Midlands, while the *Gawain* poet wrote in a dialect from further north and west, possibly Cheshire. Both borrowed many words from abroad.

Just as Old English subdivides into four main dialects, West Saxon, Kentish, Mercian, and Northumbrian, the last two constituting old Anglian, so Middle English has five, Kentish, Southern, East Midland, West Midland, and Northern. Needless to say, Modern English (since 1500) has been much enriched by borrowings from other languages. By these borrowings it went far beyond its Germanic origins and absorbed many Latinate and other words. Many of these "foreign" words are conceptually useful in dealing with abstractions, for example the word "abstractions" itself.

An Example of Early English

Here is a specimen of Middle Scots, which is not medieval Celtic at all, but a form of Northern English:

> Now we have schawin sufficientlie ineuch of the Ilis of Scotland, gif we had schawin ane thing; that is to say, nocht allanerlie wes the Ile of Thule, with all the remanent Ilis of Scotland sene by us, bot als were sene be mony Romane auctouris: for Cornelius Tacitus sayis, the Romane navy, quhilk wes send about the Ilis be command of Julius Agricola, saw this Ile of Thule, with the remanent Ilis liand thairabout. And thoucht Ptoleme writhis, that the Ile of Thule lyis amang the Ilis of Scotland, yit his writing, be provin experience, may have na faith; for Schetland lyis beyound Orknay, approechand to Noroway. Sum auctouris sayis, that Thule is the samin Ile that we call Island; for their auctouris sayis, that Thule is the last Ile of the occeane see; and sa is Island; quhilk lyis in the cauld and frosty seis beyound the cirkill artik in the north pole.

This frosty passage describing Iceland and its neighbors appears in Hector Boece's *History of Scotland,* translated from the Latin by John Bellenden and published in 1536. Its language is easily understood because it was composed nearer to our own time than true medieval English. Nevertheless it will be unhelpful in contract usage.

The quoted passage discloses old and regional spelling. More to the point, perhaps, is how words vary in meaning according to time and place. The noun "punk," for example, means, in the United States, a male criminal, usually low in the hierarchy. Earlier it meant a prostitute. There is more in the example than quaintness; word meanings changed by the passage of time are unlikely to be much trouble, but meanings transformed into something different by region can wreck contracts. "Bomb," for example, used as a colloquialism for theatrical productions means "success" in England and "failure" in the United States. Correspondence making the payment of money depend on the run of a stage play might tax the goodwill of British and American negotiators who were unaware of the point.

The best way to know English is to read its classics. Contract language comes later. Shakespeare and Milton are better training, and a passage from Jane Austen is worth twenty "Whereas" clauses.

English and Other Languages

What are the characteristics of English? Diversity is its hallmark; there is a wide range of alternatives to choose from in saying things, although the conciseness of other languages is lacking. Consequently the use of English is a creative challenge. Almost too many riches are available for selection, which leads occasionally to masterpieces but more frequently to mistakes. A chief danger is going wrong in one's choice, but indecision can be awkward as well. An apocryphal mouse equidistant between two bits of cheese starved through inability to make up his mind, just as many of us perish on grander options. English is nearly too vast to get at. The attempt often is like embracing a giantess.

A few comparisons bring out how it sprawls. In Latin, "laudatur" means "he is [being] praised." English requires three or four words here to accomplish what Latin can do in one. French in turn is not so cryptic as Latin, but admirably precise. "Dites-moi ce qui vous amuse," meaning "Tell me what amuses you," spells out "that which" instead of the English "what" and distinguishes the subject by using "qui" rather than "que." English is less refined in its distinctions, and this makes us work harder to be clear.

This is not to say that English is imprecise. All things are relative, and you find greater imprecision in other languages. Japanese, for example, stresses degrees of politeness varied to reflect the respective stations of speaker and listener. Whether nouns are singular or plural has to be determined by context; words meaning "I" or "you" often are left out because you talk up or down according to rank, and circumlocution on a grand scale is preferred to plain statement. Thus "Taberu koto ga dekimasen" means "You can't eat it," but literally it would be more like "To eat thing isn't possible." Formal Japanese used in official pronouncements can be even more baffling. "Migi konnan nari" means "The above is difficult," but "Migi konnan ari" is "We have the difficulty set forth above," and abbreviations such as "Mokogun" for "Mongolian army units" take a little guesswork. Japanese has its own riches but would be unsuitable as an international contract language.

That role has been assigned to English. How well it plays the part varies sharply from one performance to another. A good script is essential, as well as a strong director.

A Sampling of Contract Phrases

Our observations about English so far have been general in nature. Earlier we considered the Position-taking Style, so it appears logical next to examine how well the two are suited to each other. A full glossary is beyond reach, but examples of favorite contract phrases will help ease the way to fuller examination of entire negotiations and contracts. In what follows there is a listing of words and phrases that turn up in a great many documents, with comments on each one. The words and phrases are presented in plausible contract sequence, not alphabetically.

"Whereas" Everyman's idea of how a contract begins. That this is not necessarily the case has been brought out in Chapter 1, but the word is acceptable enough unless the tail begins wagging the dog. Some lawyers dislike "Whereases" and use recitation clauses so marked to distinguish them from the text of the contract. There the real issue lies; you must be careful about mixing up recitals of history with what is actually being agreed on. For example, it would be folly to write, "Whereas A admits owing B $10,000," more likely than not because the admission may later haunt one, especially if drafts are never signed and the debt is disputed. Rather less damaging would be, "Whereas the parties have engaged in a series of transactions resulting in dispute over accountings between them," or something equally noncommital. "Whereas" is acceptable, but what follows it needs particular care. "Whereas what?" is the question.

"It Is Understood and Agreed" Absurd and sometimes dangerous. There is nothing wrong with "We agree as follows" or something to that effect once at the beginning of a contract, but repetition of "It is understood and agreed" adds either nothing or something. If it adds nothing, it ought not to be said. Usually it is the case that it adds nothing, because every clause in the contract is "understood and agreed" or it would not be written into it. On the other hand, if it adds something, what it adds is a bad thing, namely an implication that other clauses not propped up by this phrase are somehow not understood or agreed on at all. "Inclusio unius est exclusio alterius" goes the Latin maxim: by including the one you exclude the other. An even worse phrase not infrequently encountered is, "It is clearly understood and agreed." How clearly, more so than with clauses merely "understood and agreed," presumably in some fuzzy manner? Further degrees of clarity offer grotesque prospects: "It is very clearly understood and agreed," or "most clearly," perhaps even "crystal clearly" as the superlative. "It is understood and agreed" ought to be banished.

"Hereinafter" A decent enough little word doing the job of six and deserving of promotion for its hard work. Without it we should have to use phrases such as "Referred to later in this document," which is long and not always meticulous since "referred to" suggests incidental mention in passing, which is not quite the flavor. "Hereinafter" frequently sets up abbreviated names for the contract parties, something very useful with German companies. Accordingly "Knightsbridge International Drapers and Fishmongers, Ltd. (hereinafter 'Knightsbridge')," is useful shorthand but it can be carried too far. A business letter saying "We are happy to be doing business again with Knightsbridge International Drapers and Fishmongers, Ltd. (hereinafter 'Knightsbridge'), and are putting our best man, Robert (hereinafter 'Bob') Luciano, on the account" belongs with Alice in Wonderland (hereinafter "Wonderland").

"Aforesaid" A revolting word that has little to recommend it. "Aforesaid" and its companion, "The said" whatever you please, accomplish nothing that cannot be dealt with by more exact reference. We can say, "The formula specified in paragraph 6 of this agreement," or even "specified above," and in the case of names we can fall back on "Knightsbridge" if the name has been sensibly tagged in the "Hereinafter" clause. That makes it unnecessary to say, "The aforesaid Knightsbridge." All that affords you is tautology, and in an age of conservation we must conserve not only resources but words as well. "Aforesaid" belongs in *Pickwick,* where it appeared at the beginning of this chapter.

"Such" A little better than "Aforesaid," although just as pompous. "Such patents," for example, makes sense if the draftsman earlier had been describing a category of patents as distinct from a series of patents identified by number. In those circumstances "such" picks up the reference to everything in the named category. Its use, however, can be overextended and disfigure style. "All such patents will be assigned" is tolerable. "Such Knightsbridge" and "Knightsbridge will become the owner of such" are not tolerable at all. They belong with our next word, which belongs in limbo.

"Same" Here we have a word that turns up in all sorts of odd places like an unwelcome guest. "The same XYZ Company" ranks no better than "the said Company," and "XYZ Company will furnish same" ranks even lower. Same what? Business people frequently misuse this word under the impression that it sounds legal. Employed properly it commits no offense, e.g., "articles in the same category." But used to create an impression, as is too frequently the case, it sounds like "Pleased to make your acquaintance" and is best abandoned.

"Including without Limitation" Useful and at times essential. Earlier we noted that mentioning certain things may exclude others by implication. Thus, "You may assign your exclusive British and Commonwealth rights" suggests that you may not, perhaps, assign other rights assuming you have any. Similarly the phrase may restrict assignment of nonexclusive rights, if any exist. These pitfalls may be avoided by phrasing such as "You may assign any and all your rights including without limitation your exclusive British and Commonwealth rights." But why specify any rights if all of them are included? Psychology is the main reason; people want specific things underscored in their contracts, and "including without limitation" or "included but not limited to" indulges this predilection. Even so there are risks, for example inadvertently excluding things in a completely different category from what you thought to have included by using the magic words. "I will reserve all remaining rights including without limitation patents and trademarks" may fail to secure rights to buy stock shares or land at prearranged prices since these are so utterly different. "Including without generic or specific limitation" may be of help there. Usually this degree of refinement will be unnecessary. "Including without limitation" should do well enough.

"Assignees and Licensees" Important words whose acceptability depends on one's point of view. "Knightsbridge, its assignees and licensees" suggests that Knightsbridge may hand you over at will to somebody else after contracts are signed. If you yourself happen to be Knightsbridge, you will want that particular right and should use the phrase. A full clause on assignability is better, but half a loaf is better than none.

"Without Prejudice" A classic. The British use this phrase all by itself, leaving the reader a little hungry. Without prejudice to what, exactly? Americans spell it out more elaborately, but if you fancy the

American way, remember "including without limitation," or you may accidentally exclude something by implication. Legal rights, for example, are not the same thing as remedies the law affords to enforce them. Thus the American might say, "Without prejudice to any of my existing or future rights or remedies." And this leads to the next phrase.

"And/or" An essential barbarism. In the preceding example we got by with the disjunctive "rights or remedies." This is not always good enough, and we run into trouble with "John or Teddy or either of them shall have the option." What about both together? "John and Teddy," perhaps, followed by "or either." Occasionally the alternatives become overwhelming, and when that happens "and/or" is convenient and generally accepted, although more detail is better.

"Shall" Do we say "John and/or Teddy shall have the option" or "will have the option"? Grammarians and/or stylists are fond of this question. Legally it should make no difference if you are consistent in using one or the other. "Shall," however, is a bit stronger than "will." Going from one to the other might suggest that one obligation is stronger somehow than another. "Shall" sounds a little like a chorus from Handel's *Messiah:* "And He shall rule for ever and ever." Perhaps one's bargaining position may determine the choice. "You shall," however, is bad form.

"Understanding" A dangerous word. If you mean "agreement" you ought to say so. If your view of affairs is that there is no agreement, "understanding" as a noun suggests the opposite—or comes close to it. It stands, in fact, as a monument to unsatisfactory compromise. The softness of the word conjures up pleasing images, but it wants teeth. "In accordance with our understanding" can be interpreted in a number of ways. This being so, the key word falls between two stools, to the satisfaction of nobody except the court lawyers.

"Notwithstanding" The usefulness of elephants is beyond dispute but is limited to special and few places. This elephantine word is helpful when you want to trample over an array of clauses to the opposite effect. It has the quality of "overriding" or "yes, but" and should be used sparingly. "Notwithstanding anything to the contrary set forth in this agreement" is good enough, provided you are not trying to override other agreements as well and forgot to say so. "Anything hereinbefore notwithstanding" is an example of less helpful phrasing. It will not prevail over clauses that come later on, and it sounds like gibberish. Elephants can do heavy work, but take care lest they trample the mahout himself.

"Effect" Here is a little word whose uses are insufficiently praised. Time and again we find language such as "We will produce" this, that, and the other, which is inaccurate because the work will be subcontracted and the promise-maker technically defaults. Somebody else does the producing. Very well, why not say, "We will produce or cause to be produced"? This is in fact often said, but it jars the ear and agreeing to "cause" anything suggests an implied obligation to sue, at one's own expense, to enforce rights against third parties to whom the work is subcontracted. Accordingly "We will effect production" straddles the point with greater skill. It suggests that we may do it or arrange that somebody else do it, without promising war if other people default.

"Profits" A verbal mousetrap. The word itself is inevitable but requires definition. "Net profits," for example, must be defined by reciting what deductions will be subtracted before net profits are computed and the shares paid. The process of doing so is like peeling layer after layer off an onion. Each layer has a name: "Net profits will be defined as they are defined in our contract with a distributor but in any event will be computed and determined only after deduction first of all production, distribution, and advertising costs and fees, local taxes, amounts reasonably allocated to overhead, travel and entertainment expenses, and profit shares payable to third parties." There you have only one example, but it brings out the onion flavor. "Gross profits" similarly needs definition. Something will be deducted first or the phrase would be "gross receipts."

"Idea" Bad for your own side but helpful against others. Ideas as such are not generally protected by law. If you submit something to a company with any hope of reward you must find better phrasing than "my idea." Perhaps "my format" or possibly "my property" is more appropriate, even though self-serving. Naturally if you can develop an idea into a format or protectable property, the more ambitious phrasing will be better justified.

"As between Us" A wallflower of a phrase that deserves greater popularity. It is useful because people are always forgetting or neglecting to mention that a great many interests may be involved in what appears to be simple dialogue. "I reserve control" over this and "You have the final power of decision over that" sound like the division of something into spheres, but frequently I am in turn controlled by my investors and you by a foreign parent company, making the language of division inaccurate. Neither of us really controls anything, at least ultimately. Thus it will be useful to say, "As between us, I control," and so on. That way nobody misrepresents his power in the course of sorting things out between two people in dialogue. Their position vis-à-vis one another is arranged, but each looks over his shoulder at absent masters.

"Spanning" Time periods are awkward things: "For a period commencing August 1 and expiring November 15" is clumsy and "From August 1 to November 15" is skeletal when reciting how long a contract obligation endures. The second is not always inadequate, and "Your services are to be exclusive to us from August 1 to November 15" does well enough in correspondence. But not everything is that simple, because during particular time periods one may be reporting for work, for example, three days out of every five, or doing something else that is within but not completely parallel to the entire time period involved. Thus it will become awkward to say, "You will render services as a consultant three days out of every five from August 1 to November 15." A happy solution, not often seen, is the word "spanning." It goes this way: "Throughout the period spanning August 1–November 15 inclusive you will render services as a consultant three days out of every five." A little counting is necessary to make it come out right, but setting up the time period "within which" is the real challenge. It will be useful to put "inclusive" at the end, as in the model sentence. Without it you may lose the day of November 15 or whatever concludes the period being spanned.

"Consultant" This is one of the most interesting words available. There may be a time when you are burdened with somebody's unwelcome child as part of a business transaction. Or you may want to engage somebody but find yourself unable to do so because of union difficulties. Tax considerations and other impediments may prevent making the person vice president in charge of sales. Most important of all, perhaps, you may wish to limit somebody's authority. In any of these circumstances, a good title may be "consultant." The consultant himself keeps his dignity, and the image conjured up should please everybody. A consultant is a senior executive, so wise that his advice is sought out but so busy that he has less than full time for one project. He smokes his pipe, straightens things out, and stays calm when others get into a flap. "Consultant" solves many problems. The word often excels the personage. De Quincey was much impressed by the title "Consul Romanus," but he lived too late to know any of them personally.

"Negotiate in Good Faith" A phrase best characterized as "a throwing up of hands." The negotiators have worked until late at night. All points but one have been worked out. The contract never will be signed without resolution of some particular impasse. What is there to do? Agree to "negotiate in good faith" on the disputed point at some later time. This is done frequently, but make no mistake about the outcome. The open point remains open. If it happens to be vital, you may have no contract at all. "Negotiate in good faith" is one of those evasions that must be used sparingly. At the right time it prevents collapse. At the wrong time it promotes it. Perhaps we can best consider it a midnight phrase, useful only in that it affords everyone a chance to rest and begin the next day with new approaches.

"Confirm" A word for Reynard the Fox. It suggests, of course, that something has been agreed to before; you are writing now only to make a record of it. "I write to confirm that you owe me $5,000" or "that you admit substantial default in delivery"; how very cunning are its varied uses. "Confirm," to be fair about it, is not always that Byzantine. Frequently we encounter it in ordinary correspondence: "Confirming your order," "Confirming the main points of our agreement," and so on. But the word contains, more than most do, an immeasurable capacity for mischief. The question is whether or not it rings true; in that sense "Confirm" becomes more than a word and ranks with dogma.

"Furnish" A handy word whose usefulness lies in the avoidance of worse alternatives. Suppose you transact to deliver a variety of elements as a package. "Deliver" leaves out, even though it may well be implied, the preliminary purchase or engagement of these elements, and at the other end it goes very far in suggesting responsibility for getting the package unscathed to where it belongs. Alternatives also may go wrong, slightly, each with its own implications. "Assign" involves legal title; "give" is lame and probably untrue; "transmit" means send; and so they go, each word or phrase a near miss. "Furnish" is sometimes useful when more popular words fall short or go too far. It has a good professional ring to it as well: "I agree to furnish all of the elements listed on Exhibit A annexed hereto and made part hereof by incorporation." Who is responsible for nondelivery and related questions can be dealt with in separate clauses. "Furnish" avoids jumping the gun. It keeps away from what ought to be treated independently but fills up enough space to stand firm. The word is good value.

"Right but Not Obligation" One of the most splendid phrases available. Sometimes the grant of particular rights carries with it by implication a duty to exploit them. Authors, for example, often feel betrayed by their publishers, who have various rights "but do nothing about them." Royalties dwindle as a result; and this situation, whether or not it reflects real delinquency, recurs in a variety of industries and court cases. Accordingly it well suits the grantee of rights to make clear at the very beginning that he may abandon them. This possibility is more appropriately dealt with in separate clauses reciting the consequences. Still, contracts have been known to contain inconsistent provisions, and preliminary correspondence may not even reach the subject of rights that are just gathering dust. A quick phrase helps keep you out of trouble: "The right but not the obligation." Thus, "We shall have the right but not the obligation to grant sublicenses in Austria" ("But if we fail," as the Macbeths say to one another, "we fail"). Even this magic phrase has its limitations because good faith may require having a real go at exploiting the rights in question. Nevertheless "right but not obligation" is useful, so much so as to become incantation and be said whenever circumstance allows it. If the other side challenges these words, it will be better to know this at once and work out alternatives or end negotiations completely.

"Exclusive" A word too easily associated with high fashion. Its importance in Contract English is vast, and its omission creates difficulties in a good many informal drafts. Exclusivity as a contract term means that somebody is barred from dealing with others in a specified area. Typically an employment may be exclusive in that the employee may not work for anyone else, or a license may be exclusive in the sense that no competing licenses will be issued. Antitrust problems cluster around exclusive arrangements but they are not all automatically outlawed. It follows that one ought to specify whether or not exclusivity is part of many transactions. If not, the phrase "nonexclusive" does well enough. On the other hand, if a consultant is to be engaged solely by one company, or a distributorship awarded to nobody else except X, then "exclusive" is a word that deserves recitation. "Exclusive right but not obligation" is an example that combines two phrases discussed here. The linking of concepts is a step in building a vocabulary of Contract English.

"Solely on Condition that" One of the few phrases that can be considered better than its shorter counterparts. Why not just "if"? Because "if" by itself leaves open the possibility of other contingencies: "If Baker delivers 1,000 barrels I will buy them" is unclear if you will buy them only from Baker. It closes no doors. Therefore what about "only if"? Sometimes this works out, but not always. "I will buy 1,000 barrels only if Baker delivers them" is an example of "only if" going fuzzy. One possible meaning is "not more than 1,000 barrels" with "only" assimilated to the wrong word. Here then a more elaborate phrase is justified. "I will buy 1,000 barrels solely on condition that Baker deliver them" makes everything clear. Similarly, "You will prosper solely on condition that you study Contract English" says what it means to say, although what it means to say may be something of an exaggeration.

"Subject to" One of the great classics, like Jane Austen. Few contracts can do without it. Many promises can be made good only if certain things occur. The right procedure is to spell out these plausible impediments to the degree that you can reasonably foresee them. "We will deliver these subject to our receiving adequate supplies"; "I will employ you subject to receiving adequate clearances"; "Our agreement is subject to the laws of Connecticut"; "Subject to circumstances beyond our control including without limitation"—the phrase runs through Contract English like a main theme in a symphony. Elsewhere it has little justification. "Long live the Prime Minister" is a good phrase; but if a voice in the crowd adds, "Subject to the conditions set forth in my political treatise," it mars the sentiment and invites the attention of security personnel. "Subject to" is superb, but it should be used subject to common sense.

Foreign and Esoteric Words

Every now and then a scholarly phrase becomes accepted in business usage. "Pro rata" and "pari passu" are Latin expressions but concern money. "Pro rata" proves helpful when payments are to be in a proportion reflecting earlier formulas in a contract. "Pari passu" is used when several people are paid at the same level or time out of a common fund. Latin, however, is by no means our only source. "Force majeure" is a French phrase used by many to mean circumstances beyond their control.

English itself has plenty of rare words whose meticulous use adds a little spice to a succession of dull dinners. One example is "eschew"; how many times we see people struggling with negatives such as "and we agree not to produce (whatever it is) for a period of X." A much happier phrase would be "we will eschew production." There may well be a telephone call asking what this word means, but the experiment will have enriched the transaction with a touch of style. Too much style, however, seems eccentric and better suited to Elizabethan drama. Therefore rare words should be used only once in a long while. Whoever uses them sparingly appears reliable, but with hidden depths.

A Short Diatribe against Passives

This chapter has consisted largely of contract words and phrases accompanied by brief essays evaluating their usefulness. The words and phrases are only samplings and are presented mainly to conduce thinking suited to the Position-taking Style. It will be wrong, however, to bring our list to an end without mention of a more general problem that arises in connection with no fixed word pattern at all. It arises, rather, from using too many passives. Such phrases as "The material will be delivered," "The start date is to be decided," and

"The figures must be approved" are an obscure pageant leaving unsettled who it is that delivers, who decides, and who does the approving. Which side is it to be? Lawsuits are the plausible outcome of leaving it all unsettled. Too many passives are a blight on English generally. In contracts, more specifically, they can destroy an entire harvest. "You will deliver" is better by virtue of being active. "Must be approved by us" is passive but has at least the virtue of identifying the one who approves. Of course, "must be approved by us" violates other canons by virtually requiring that we approve something. "We shall have the right but not the obligation to approve" is less unfortunate. Be that as it may, passives are bad style, and if they go all the way through without adding something like "by you" or "by us," they are intolerable. Once in a long while you may find them used purposely to leave something unresolved. In those circumstances they will be in a class with "negotiate in good faith," which we examined earlier. In the main, however, obscurity is a vice, and the passive is its handmaiden.

The Art of Penetrating Disguise

If you met a friend dressed in eighteenth century costume you would still know that it was K or X indulging himself for some private purpose. Some of our words and phrases also appear in disguise. The trick is to recognize them in altered costume. Thus if somebody writes, "My list is not exhaustive," we recognize "including without limitation" in different form, while "You will be unable to act in the same capacity for others" is "exclusive" poured into a new bottle but not quite full, because "same capacity" leaves open the possibility of different capacities. There are shades and degrees, but you must see through disguises and know who wears them.

Isolated words and phrases mean very little. In context they mean a great deal, and in the special context of contractual undertakings they mean everything. This is why they must be considered in terms of common law rules relating to contracts. English poetry is engendered by fancy. Contract English is prose engendered by plan.

And it includes, without limitation, the right but not the obligation to select words from a wide variety of verbal implements and write clearly, accurately, and/or with style.

CHAPTER THREE

The Analysis of Contract Proposals

Going beyond fundamentals is the critical stage in any study. Somebody learning Greek, for example, may have memorized the alphabet and mastered a few conjugations, but translating a simple passage from Xenophon is something else again.

Contract English is no different. Thus far we have considered some basic rules and sample phrases usually communicated, as befits their fragmentary nature, by cable or telex or even in conversation. Bits and pieces, however, take you just so far; ultimately someone weaves them together into a document, and then something more is required than merely being on guard. When this happens we leave the stage, take off our demolition costumes, and reenter as architects.

Two phases ensue: in the first, we react to proposed contracts drafted by somebody else, and in the second, which presents greater challenges, we compose our own. This chapter deals with the first and easier phase, since we have just barely left the nest. Before going on, however, a few notions about structure and style deserve mention.

The Importance of Sequence

There are people who like books and films made up, as dreams are, of things jumbled out of rational order, sudden changes of theme, voices whispering in endless corridors. This surrealistic style of writing, however, is unsuited to contracts. We for our part have to be old-fashioned and look for a beginning, a middle, and an end.

And yet how often the surrealistic is inflicted on us when the mail arrives! The document begins with a set of tables, or a schedule of rates, or a reference to something which turns out to be missing, and we must look very hard for any contract basis to it, which in one form or another must always be that A promises this and B promises that. Even in this age of computers, a comprehensible series of mutual promises is what makes a contract. When they prove elusive, surrealism has gone too far and ought to be sent packing back to the arts, where it properly belongs.

A good contract reads like a classic story. It narrates, in orderly sequence, that I do this and you do that, and perhaps too that if certain events occur, the outcome is changed to be thus and so. All of the rate cards, charts, and other reference material ought to be ticked off one after the other according to the sense of it. Tables of figures, code words, and mystical references are almost insulting unless organized and defined. Without organization they baffle; without definition they entrap. Perhaps it is too much to expect anything as clear as "The Company agrees to insure the named premises against the risks listed in paragraph 2 and in the amounts recited in paragraph 3," but when the opening contract paragraph begins "See Rider X" (which turns out to be Schedule Q anyway) the reader has cause for pique.

Whether something can be done about it depends on the bargaining position. In a strong stance, one can send back the offending document and request a substitute document in comprehensible English. Otherwise a series of questions may be put by letter, and the replies often will have contractual force if the document is later contested.

Again, beware if the basic undertakings in a contract are hard to find.

Drafting American Style

Americanism is a subject that looms large in many international transactions. There are people who resist using English because they consider it a colonial language or "American English" because it enlarges American influence abroad. In 1974 *The Times* of London reported a French-Dutch proposal to print EEC documents in Latin. This proposal was later conceded to be a joke and was withdrawn; since then the cause has had few champions. It seems too bad in a way, since a brush-up in Latin might be a good thing for everyone, but English as an international language seems destined to be with us for a long time.

The cultural and political aspects of American influence are scarcely germane to our subject. What is very much so, however, is something a great deal more specific: the American style of writing contracts. Here a genuine issue arises, and it is much debated.

American contracts generally are more elaborate than others. That puts the case in a nutshell. The Americans try to cover all of the plausible eventualities, and they consume more space in doing so. The British generally go the opposite way; they like their contracts short, matter-of-fact, and confined to setting down the main points. The Americans dislike leaving things up in the air. As soon as one point is settled they raise the question, "But what happens if . . . ?"

The larger part of the world follows the British style in these matters. Reasons for the difference in approach very likely include the relative complexity of the American industrial structure, the magnitude of its stakes, and the large role played by lawyers in the United States. Whatever the reasons, the results are what count. Which is better?

Ideally a clear and concise short form written without lawyers has a surface attraction. Most of the troublesome possibilities never will arise; if they do, goodwill solves everything. We trust each other; besides, if we try spelling everything out, the legal fees will be higher. This is how many Europeans see it.

The best American counterargument is that anything worth doing is worth doing well. They have a point. Sometimes prolix, occasionally guilty of "overkill," American contracts in the main are more sophisticated than others. Perhaps it all depends on whether one prefers Beethoven or plainsong.

Self-Interrogation Disciplines

We conclude that orderly sequence is essential and that the suitability of elaborate American-style contracts is a matter of taste and judgment. These reflections shape our initial reaction to contracts submitted for our approval. The next step is to consider ways of undertaking more detailed analysis. First impressions never can overcome the small print.

Contract analysis consists of three principal phases, the first being to form a general impression, before even reading the document, of what ought to be in it and what the danger areas are likely to be. This phase is almost subconscious, but the next two are more studied. The second consists in reading the document through against a mental checklist of points, and the third in going through it clause by clause, making notes of everything that seems wrong, or unclear, or worth mentioning to somebody else even if clear and correct. This third phase of course is the most important, and it usually requires a number of readings.

Now in doing all this you will find it useful to keep asking yourself questions as you go along. This is what is meant by self-interrogation disciplines; no matter how smoothly the prose flows, it will be indispensable to keep prodding youself mentally, not only for the purpose of keeping awake but to be sure nothing gets by.

This entire thought process is best examined as the stream of consciousness of that favorite fiction of the law, the average reasonably prudent man, whose initial reactions are reproduced here after the letter "Q" for question and whose provisional solutions are suggested after the letter "A" for answer. Let us consider him in circumstances as they really occur, reacting imperfectly to an imperfect contract. Imperfection, however, is something better than idiocy, and we shall give our protagonist credit for some minimal knowledge of Contract English.

By way of preliminary exercise, and to establish the format, we consider this sample text:

> We hereby grant to you and your assigns the right to enter upon our premises at 203 Church Street and to photograph our conduct of regular business at those premises on any or all the dates specified on Schedule A.

Q: What about exclusivity? My rights mean nothing if others can do the same thing.

A: Add "exclusive" before the word "right."

Q: But doesn't that still leave open the possibility that others can do the same thing at different times, that is to say, on dates which are not listed on Schedule A? This would be nearly as bad as the other.

A: Add at the end, "Throughout the entire period spanning the first and last dates listed on Schedule A, no similar rights will be granted to any other person, firm, or corporation."

Q: But suppose competing rights have in fact already been granted? Perhaps a warranty that they haven't might help, or take out "no similar rights," etc., and say instead, "no other person may have access to your premises." But this is absurd and bars even the milkman. Think of a better way of saying it.

And so on. This unsolved fragment establishes the format. Now let us proceed to the analysis of Contract English in a complete document.

A Foreign Distributorship

In this extended example a Vermont corporation (hereinafter sometimes referred to as "Vermont") holds the exclusive right to distribute outside Japan and to appoint subdistributors of an unpatented ski lift called "Yukitori," which means "Snow Bird," pursuant to agreement with the Japanese owners (hereinafter "Japan"). Vermont writes to a company in Scotland ("Scotland") asking carefully, in the best Position-taking Style, whether Scotland would be interested in taking on the sales of Yukitori in the UK. There is no nonsense about it and Scotland writes back expressing interest instead of cabling "We accept," since the Scots wish to be in this more advanced chapter rather than appear at the beginner's section of this book. After proper negotiations Vermont and Scotland come to an agreement, whereupon Japan hears about it and sends Vermont a proposed form of contract to be used with the Scots. The Japanese invite comments before Vermont issues it. Accordingly we now are positioned for contract analysis.

In what follows we consider the English text from Japan, annotating it with Vermont's analysis. Self-interrogation notes after each paragraph reflect what goes on in the Vermont reader's mind.

Pitfalls Sight Unseen

Before reading the document at all he anticipates these problems:

1. Danger. A ski lift suggests accidents. I have to be sure that Scotland bears all the risk. While thinking about this I had better look up my signed contract with Japan as well and see what sort of backing they give me if the machine breaks.
2. Exclusivity. Am I giving the Scots exclusivity, and, if so, for the entire UK? Possibly the UK area would be academic because I hear very little about skiing in Cornwall.
3. Improvements. Do I give them distributorship of future improved models or just Yukitori as it appears in the present catalogue?
4. Name. Be careful about their use of the trademark.

And so on. These reflections are special to this transaction. Naturally the financial terms are uppermost, but that goes without saying.

Vermont reads the contract. Then its head official considers it paragraph by paragraph, as follows.

DISTRIBUTION AGREEMENT

> XYZ, Inc., a Vermont corporation located in the United States of America, having offices at 122 Maple Street, Manchester, Vt. (hereinafter called "Vermont"), as exclusive licensee for the distribution outside Japan of ski lifts and related equipment, and ———— (specify corporation), a corporation having offices at ———— (specify place of incorporation) (hereinafter called "Scotland"), hereby make this agreement for the purpose of selling, distributing, installing, and servicing Yukitori ski lifts and related equipment in ———— (specify territory). For this purpose the parties agree as follows:

Q: The preamble seems harmless enough but a few points are worrisome. For example, is it enough to designate us as "exclusive licensee?" That might be inadequate if we had to sue interlopers in our own name.

A: A Scottish legal opinion may be required on points of that kind. Still, there seems very little we can do about it now, since the Scots are unlikely to change their laws to accommodate me.

Q: Why must I say that the purpose of this agreement is for selling and doing these other things with the ski lifts, especially when we mention "related equipment"? I may be giving them an option on new models before even getting into the body of the contract. "Related equipment" is an Alarm Phrase. I am making a note to keep watching for it as I go along. There is no point giving away more rights than I have to at this stage.

A: It says too much.

Q: Even if I confine their territory to Scotland or the UK, does that prevent them from selling abroad? It seems to, but I need European legal advice on the monopoly law. Again, the best I can do now is confine the territory and hope it will stand up.

A: Note this for the Japanese.

1. Distributorship

a. Vermont grants to Scotland for the period of this agreement and subject to the terms and conditions thereof the exclusive right to sell, distribute, install, and service Yukitori ski lifts and related equipment in ———— (area) (hereinafter "the Territory").

b. Scotland's rights under paragraph *a* above are not assignable or otherwise transferable; provided, however, that Scotland may appoint assistant or subsidiary dealers in the Territory for the purpose of selling, distributing, installing, and servicing Yukitori ski lifts and related equipment. Scotland agrees to advise Vermont in writing of the names and addresses of any proposed or subsidiary dealers and the appointment thereof shall be subject to the approval of Vermont. Scotland agrees to be responsible for the observation by any such assistant or subsidiary dealer of the terms and conditions of this agreement and further agrees that, unless Vermont otherwise instructs Scotland, all orders to Vermont for ski lifts and related equipment shall be placed through Scotland and Scotland shall be responsible for payment therefor.

Q: They have an exclusive right to sell our equipment, but what prevents them from selling rival equipment?

A: Balance this by a parallel obligation to deal exclusively in Yukitori equipment. We don't want to be undercut.

Q: What happens if they install or service negligently?

A: Ski lifts can be dangerous. Again, they need some obligation to match their rights. Probably this point will be dealt with later in the contract as I read on, but I am making a note of it.

Q: My approval of their appointed subsidiary dealers ought to be in writing so that nobody can say we approved someone in a telephone conversation. Further, saying that Scotland "agrees to be responsible" for making these other people observe this contract is vague. Policing them should be at no cost to ourselves. Further, we need some tougher English to make Scotland indemnify us if their subsidiaries breach. We also need a right to proceed directly against these assistants and subsidiaries if this is available under Scots law.

A: We had better line up a good law firm in Scotland.

Q: "Related equipment" bothers me. Does Japan realize that we may be obligating ourselves to give Scotland improved ski lifts and even articles which are not ski lifts at all? Japan might start manufacturing skis, for example, or brandy flasks or mittens. These might be considered "related equipment."

A: I will certainly take this up with Japan. My suggestion will be to confine our grant of rights to the Yukitori ski lift as it appears in the present catalogue. If the Scots want more, let them negotiate for it.

> 2. Term
>
> The initial term of this Agreement shall be ——— years commencing ———. At the end of the ——— year period, the Agreement shall automatically be renewed for additional one-year periods unless one party hereto notifies the other of its intention to terminate the Agreement at the end of the current period by notice in writing delivered before the expiration of such period. For purposes of this Agreement a year shall constitute the twelve-month period beginning ———. Scotland agrees to purchase during each year of this Agreement at least the minimum dollar amounts of Yukitori ski lifts and equipment set forth in paragraph 3 below.

Q: Instead of automatic renewal year to year it might be safer to have the contract expire unless renewed. Shall we?

A: The question is whether we prefer the risk of forgetting to renew or forgetting to call it off. In any event the word "unless" fails to spell out as clearly as I should like to do that termination follows nonrenewal, and "intention to terminate" is very weak as well. Some road or other was paved with good intentions.

Q: The last sentence about a minimum order belongs in a separate paragraph. It seems a key thought, and the more I look at it, the more I think it could be improved. What happens, for example, if Scotland fails to purchase the minimum and we terminate?

A: Clarify to the effect that Scotland, in those circumstances, would owe the balance and still be subject to termination. Certainly we can terminate in the normal course, but their failure to make the required purchase would be a breach and enable us to terminate earlier.

Q: Isn't it still weak, talking about minimum purchases payable at some indeterminate time?

A: I assume an advance or down payment on signing is provided for later on. Worth noting.

Q: There is also a possibility of our own default. How do I know we can fill even the minimum orders?

A: Make another note and look sharp for escape clauses later on.

3. Orders

a. All orders placed by Scotland under this Agreement shall be subject to acceptance in writing by Vermont. Vermont agrees to fill Scotland's orders promptly insofar as practical and consistent with production and shipping scheduling, but shall not be responsible for delays caused by strikes, civil strife, acts of God, or event or acts beyond the control of Vermont. Upon Vermont's written acceptance thereof, orders shall become binding contracts by Scotland to purchase Yukitori ski lifts and related equipment on the terms set forth herein.

b. Scotland agrees and guarantees to purchase during each year of this Agreement at least the minimum dollar amounts of Yukitori ski lifts and related equipment as set forth below:

Twelve (12)-Month Period Ending ———	*Amount of Minimum Purchase*
	$
	$
	$
	$
	$

For each year subsequent to ———, Scotland agrees and guarantees to purchase a minimum dollar amount equal to one hundred per cent (100%) of the actual amount purchased by Scotland during the immediately preceding year. For purposes of this provision purchases may be credited against minimum amounts at the time of placing of orders; provided, however, that Scotland shall be given no credit against minimum purchases for any order which is subsequently canceled. An initial order for Yukitori ski lifts and related equipment in the amount of ——— shall be due upon execution of this Agreement.

Q: I don't like all these names. I'm not even sure the Scots are distributors; I thought people who sold on commission were distributors and people who bought for resale were brokers. Is this important?

A: Put this to the lawyers when they review the contract.

Q: I see the escape clause I was looking for in 3*a*. Is it sufficient?

A: Probably, but is it clear that it covers acts of God in Japan as well as Vermont?

Q: If we accept an order, is Scotland liable to pay us the full amount even if they can't collect from the customer?

A: We may be something like a third party beneficiary to a contract between the customer and Scotland. I understand the UK doesn't protect that status. Whatever the status, it would be a good thing to tighten it up and make Scotland pay us in full whether or not they collect.

Q: In 3*b* the language about 100% of previous purchases could be more effective if we added an absolute minimum purchase requirement. The point about their making good the balance comes in again here.

A: Look further.

Q: At the end I see a provision implying that money changes hands on signing. Is this the missing link I was looking for?

A: No. All they assure us on signing is a minimum "initial order," which we have anyway. Initial order and initial payment are scarcely the same thing. In plain Contract English the better phrase would be something like, "As a nonreturnable advance against minimum orders, Scotland is paying Vermont $X simultaneously with signing this agreement." We must take this up with Japan as a policy matter.

4. Price

Vermont will furnish Scotland with a current net export price list FOB Manchester, Vt. Although Vermont has in the past and expects in the future to follow the policy of an annual price schedule on each ——— (insert date), current price schedules may be modified at any time. Changes in said price list shall be effective upon mailing of notice thereof by Vermont to Scotland. The effective price for any ski lift or related equipment ordered by Scotland shall be as specified on the price list, which is effective as of the date of acceptance by Vermont of the order for said ski lift or related equipment.

Q: Does our right to change price schedules protect us against currency fluctuations?

A: Not really, once orders have been accepted.

Q: Isn't the opening clause of the second sentence bad English?

A: Yes. Add "followed" after "past." Otherwise there is a verb missing.

Q: Does "modified at any time" protect us in terms of changing prices?

A: Not very well. These passives are always unclear. Make a note to add "by Vermont" after "modified" to clarify who does the modifying. For that matter, "modified" is a weak word for increasing our prices. How about "changed" or "increased or decreased at Vermont's sole discretion?" I think "modified" is polite but unclear.

> 5. PAYMENTS
>
> Scotland will establish for any purchase an applicable irrevocable letter of credit in favor of Vermont's bank within ten (10) days after receipt of order confirmation from Vermont in the amount of the order confirmation. The letter of credit must be confirmed by a U.S. bank and for the entire amount of each shipment of order when placed. The letter of credit shall allow thirty (30) days negotiation time from the day of order's confirmed shipping date. A letter of credit requirement list with specific documentation shall be attached as Appendix A to this agreement.

Q: Does this payment procedure solve the problems noted earlier?

A: Not really. It creates several new ones, for example "must be confirmed by a U.S. bank." There we have another passive, but this one is rather peculiar. Suppose the U.S. bank won't confirm?

Q: Then Scotland must be in breach.

A: It sounds right, but something in this entire pay structure seems loose. The problem is less what the paper says than what it doesn't say. Nowhere do I get the feeling of real "teeth"—that Scotland commits to pay Vermont a minimum of $X no matter what. They pay us so much on signing and the rest by the end of the year, whether or not they collect. If we terminate, they still owe the balance for that year. The bank machinery is just a specified way of implementing. If that goes wrong, Scotland still has to pay. Let them get Bank of England approval to pay in dollars. Let all these commitments be absolutely clear. I must write to Japan about this.

Q: Anything else here?

A: The last sentence confuses me. If the list is ready, it should be attached now. Where it says "shall be attached," we may have an incomplete document, with what results I don't know. The phrase ought to be in the present tense: "is attached."

6. Shipment

Vermont will supply the Yukitori ski lifts and related equipment ordered by Scotland crated for shipment FOB Manchester, Vt. At Scotland's request Vermont will arrange for shipment of said ski lifts and related equipment, all costs associated therewith to be for Scotland's account and to be paid in accordance with Article 5 hereof, provided, however, that irrespective of which party makes the shipping arrangements, except as provided below, title and risk of loss or damage shall pass from Vermont to Scotland upon delivery of the ski lift or related equipment to the shipping company or Scotland's representative for shipment. If any item is short-shipped or missed-shipped or incorrectly shipped in the case where Vermont has made the shipping arrangements, Vermont agrees to replace those items as promptly as possible free of charge and freight prepaid to Scotland's destination.

Q: I still worry about "related equipment."

A: The point was made earlier. In writing to Japan, mention that it comes up all through the contract.

Q: Does all of this paragraph put the risk of damage or loss on Scotland?

A: Yes, but the last part weakens it somewhat. Perhaps we ought to be liable if things go wrong only through our negligence.

Q: But if a ski lift never gets there, is it sensible to absolve ourselves and expect them to pay?

A: See paragraph 3 above. Perhaps we might pay back a fair portion of the purchase price if we received it or, better still, apply that amount as a credit to Scotland against the next order. This will take some negotiation.

Q: But is that safe for our side?

A: Insurance comes into it. I'm making a note to check our insurance coverage and the Japanese contract on these points.

7. Scotland's Promotional and Other Activities

a. Scotland will actively promote the sale of Yukitori ski lifts and equipment and to this end it will advertise Yukitori ski lifts with signs at its place of business and other common advertising sources. Scotland also promises to display Yukitori ski lifts in local recreational shows and local home shows and promote to its best ability Yukitori ski lifts nationwide.

b. Scotland agrees that it will not, during the period of this Agreement, directly or indirectly engage in the sale, distribution, installation, or servicing of ski lifts and related equipment which are sold in competition with said Yukitori ski lifts and equipment.

c. Scotland hereby covenants and agrees neither (1) to advertise the Yukitori ski lifts and related equipment for sale outside the Territory, nor (2) to establish or maintain a branch office or dealership or to appoint an assistant or subsidiary dealer outside the Territory for the sale or distribution of said ski lifts and equipment, nor (3) to establish or maintain a distribution warehouse located outside the Territory for distribution of said ski lifts and equipment outside the Territory. Notwithstanding the foregoing, the parties agree that nothing herein shall prohibit the sale of said ski lifts and equipment by Scotland from within to outside the Territory or prohibit sale of said ski lifts and equipment from outside to within the Territory by Vermont distributors from other territories to the extent that the freedom to make such sales outside distributorship territories is required by the applicable law.

Q: Who pays for the advertising in 7*a?*

A: Let's add a clause saying they do.

Q: Does 7*a* give them too much leeway in the use of our name?

A: Probably. I imagine a later clause will take care of that. Possibly this one should read that Scotland will do all this promotion "subject to" the later provision, if I find it. This is worth a note.

Q: What are "common advertising sources?"

A: This is quibbling. Still, it may be worth asking Japan if they expect some kind of minimal advertising budget and where it ought to be spent.

Q: Doesn't 7*b* solve an earlier problem by precluding Scotland from dealing in rival products?

A: Yes, I can strike out the previous note when I read all of this through. The only trouble is that Scotland agrees here not to engage in "the sale, distribution, installation, or servicing" of a competitive product, using the very words in the clause granting them rights to Yukitori. But they are not precluded from doing other things that compete with us, such as manufacturing somebody else's ski lift or even endorsing it. Maybe the present language prevents that, but it ought to be tightened. I don't think Japan would be amused if our distributor found a way to help the competition. "Will not in any way be connected with" might help.

Q: What about Scotland's assistant or subsidiary dealers who subdistribute?

A: I nearly missed that one. They ought to be similarly prevented from dealing with the opposition. We must put into our Scotland contract that their contracts with these other people will prohibit that kind of thing. Also Scotland's directors and principal officers; I won't want them doing competitive side ventures.

Q: Can you enforce these provisions in Scotland's contracts with third parties?

A: I don't know. When I read to the end it will probably say whose law applies.

Q: Will *7c* stand up?

A: It has the sound of an attempt to avoid antitrust pitfalls under European law. Whoever wrote that was aware of the problem. I think Japan should tell us whether they had it researched or whether we ought to have it done.

Q: At whose cost?

A: At theirs, naturally.

8. WARRANTY

All merchandise sold by Vermont to Scotland shall be subject to the standard warranty issued by Vermont on said merchandise. Except as provided below, Scotland agrees to sell Yukitori ski lifts and related equipment only on the basis of said standard Vermont warranty and promises to make no representations relating to warranty other than those set forth in said standard Vermont warranty. To the extent required by local safety standards, law, and building codes in the Territory, it is Scotland's obligation to modify the warranty given to Scotland's customers to conform hereto; provided, however, that no such modification may be made without the prior written approval of Vermont.

Q: What does our "standard warranty" say?

A: That will be the first thing to find out since we may be liable on it. I assume it makes Japan liable and not us. We're only a distributor. If a ski lift breaks it isn't our fault.

Q: Anything else?

A: Rewrite this to say that we aren't making any warranties to anyone except those that appear in the standard. And it would be a good idea to add that we can change our standard form wherever we want to. That helps Japan too.

Q: Even though the clause makes Scotland responsible for certain changes, subject to our approval?

A: Certainly. There is no inconsistency in saying they must, and we may if we choose. Let's try it anyhow.

Q: Isn't something still missing?

A: Yes, I should like some warranties from Scotland to our side to the effect that they are free to make this agreement, that they know of no claims, and so on.

Q: Doesn't this open the door to their demanding warranties direct from us to them?

A: Those must come from the Japanese. We can only warrant and represent that we are the distributor. We don't make Yukitori.

9. FINANCIAL STATEMENT

Scotland will furnish Vermont with a financial statement covering its operation within sixty (60) days after the close of each fiscal year.

Q: Something is missing, isn't it?

A: This doesn't go far enough. I think we need the usual right to inspect their books and records at usual business hours, copies of accountings they receive from their sublicensees, and all that.

10. PRODUCT MODIFICATION

Vermont may change the design of its ski lifts and related equipment at any time without notice to Scotland; such changes shall not constitute a basis for any claim against Vermont or any order cancellation.

Q: It is plausible that we can change the design of something that was ordered and make them accept it?

A: The language is ambiguous, but I worry more about the recurring point that we own and don't have to give them any rights in improved models.

11. INSPECTION

Vermont shall have reasonable access to Scotland's place of business and inventory stock to ascertain Scotland's compliance with this Agreement. It is Vermont's right to appoint a third party for such inspection purposes. Scotland also agrees to cooperate in permitting and obtaining permission for Vermont representatives to inspect Yukitori ski lifts and related equipment which have been installed or are in the process of being installed.

Q: Intuitively I sense a problem here.

A: The danger is that if we inspect under this paragraph, and approve everything, Scotland may say later on that we waived our rights if something goes wrong. We need some position-taking language that we aren't waiving anything or enlarging our warranties even if we inspect and approve. This kind of situation is trappy.

12. TRADEMARK AND TRADE NAME USE

a. Scotland acknowledges that Vermont is the owner of the trade name "YUKITORI" and the trademarks "YUKITORI" and "YUKITORI BANZAI." Scotland agrees to use such name and marks only in accordance with paragraph *b* below and will not attempt to register such name or marks in its own name either during the period or after the termination of this Agreement.

b. Vermont hereby grants to Scotland for the period of this Agreement the right to use the name "YUKITORI" and the trademarks "YUKITORI" and "YUKITORI BANZAI" in connection with its sales, distribution, installation, and servicing of Yukitori ski lifts and related equipment purchased under this Agreement and its advertising and public relations material related thereto. Scotland agrees that Vermont shall have the right to approve advertising and public relations material as issued from time to time. Scotland agrees to identify itself as an authorized distributor of Yukitori ski lifts and related equipment in connection with all activities related thereto and not to use any other trademark or name to identify said ski lifts and equipment. Scotland agrees not to use said name or marks in any manner that might indicate Scotland was other than an authorized distributor acting as an independent contractor and will not use the terms "YUKITORI" and "YUKITORI BANZAI" or any term confusingly similar thereto in its corporate name or in connection with any products other than those purchased under this Agreement.

Q: In technical areas like this one, don't we need British and American legal advice before even commenting on the business aspects?

A: Yes, and a look at our contract with Japan as well. I notice, though, that it says Scotland can't register but doesn't quite say who can, or spell out what happens if third parties infringe.

Q: The rest of the contract is "boilerplate," dealing with provisions for sending notice, what happens if the Scots go bankrupt, and all that. Shall we send it to our lawyers with these notes before writing to Japan?

A: Not quite so fast. I see provisions about quality control and technical assistance at Scotland's cost. This is very good, but our notes must emphasize that we don't waive anything by exercising these rights, that we own any trade secrets and know-how that develop even if they devise it, that we can assign the contract, that Scotland pays all maintenance and servicing costs, and that our servicing manuals in no way increase our liability. Most of all, the insurance has to be coordinated.

Q: What law applies?

A: I see a clause at the end specifying Vermont law.

Q: Does that help?

A: I don't know. It sounds more congenial than Japanese or Scots law but we need advice on that. Ultimately we may have to give way and use Scotland's laws whether we like it or not. I worry about our termination rights no matter what the contract says. Some of the European countries make it difficult getting rid of somebody.

Q: Then we need foreign legal opinions, not just advice from our own lawyer?

A: Definitely. This form is for international use. If we appoint distributors in Switzerland, we will certainly need advice on Swiss law.

Following Through

At first reading, this chronicle of an official's thought process suggests two things: that the official is a sullen type and that dealing with Contract English involves looking in a number of directions at the same time. The first notion is unfair; our Vermonter is protecting his company and the Japanese manufacturers, in that order, but without deception or dishonor. He is merely cautious and what the Americans call "hard-nosed." The second impression, that you must see everything going on at the same time, is correct. Contract English requires a sense of absent words and parties, not merely what appears at hand.

This chapter most fittingly concludes with some brief reflections on what Vermont must do next. They will take legal advice and then write to the Japanese, enclosing their contract suggestions as requested. They will have to be careful, however, even though Japan is theoretically on the same side. Nothing in the Vermont letter must abandon or weaken any rights vis-à-vis Japan.

And this brings us back to the Position-taking Style. It will not be good enough beginning, "Dear Mr. Higashikuni, the proposed contract with Scotland exposes us to liability in a number of ways that cause concern here." This beginning is undiplomatic, but, worse still, it violates some of our basic canons. The fatal word is "us"; even if that means Japan as well, it includes Vermont as one of the parties at risk if something goes wrong and may well weaken Vermont's position under the Japanese contract which made Japan responsible for misfortune. A better opening would be, "In accordance with your request we have reviewed the- proposed contract with Scotland, and we enclose a memorandum of points designed to give you better protection. One of our recommendations is that you take foreign legal advice on the issues raised."

That points more helpfully at where the risk lies and who pays for its removal. Once this position is sorted out, the Americans and Japanese take up joint positions facing Scotland, and when the Scotland contract is signed, all three join forces and may live happily ever after. If not, Contract English will help ensure that any disputes will remain civilized.

With these optimistic reflections we conclude this chapter on the analysis of contracts and turn our attention to something more challenging still—the art of composing them. Circumstances change, and the critic turns author.

CHAPTER FOUR

Drafting Step by Step

The composition of agreements in Contract English is a creative act. This being so, it has occurred to many an industrialist who fancies himself gifted with a flair for words that he can draft contracts without legal help. That this view is overly optimistic is proved by experience, but we would all be in a better position to accept that if we could see before us one of the greatest writers of all time making a botch of an important contract. And we can.

One of the most famous contracts in world literature is the document in which Faust sells his soul to the Devil. Fortunately we possess a version of it in English, and the author is Shakespeare's rival for magnificence, the great Christopher Marlowe. In Scene V of *The Tragical History of Doctor Faustus,* Marlowe presents this text:

> On these conditions following:
>
> First, that Faustus may be a spirit in form and substance.
>
> Secondly, that Mephistophilis shall be his servant, and be by him commanded.
>
> Thirdly, that Mephistophilis shall do for him, and bring him whatsoever he desires.
>
> Fourthly, that he shall be in his chamber or house invisible.
>
> Lastly, that he shall appear to the said John Faustus at all times, in what shape and form soever he please.

> I, John Faustus of Wittenberg, Doctor, by these presents, do give both body and soul to Lucifer prince of the east, and his minister Mephistophilis; and further grant unto them, that, four-and-twenty years being expired, and these articles above-written being inviolate, full power to fetch or carry the said John Faustus, body and soul, flesh and blood, into their habitation wheresoever. By me, John Faustus.

Poor work; how limp and lame this contract reads will be instantly perceived by the reader. Is Lucifer a third party beneficiary? What if Faustus chooses to be visible at times rather than invisible? And what if he elects to be invisible out-of-doors, not merely in his house or chamber? Even Marlowe must have sensed that the instrument was defective. Earlier he calls the contract a "deed," but later on his play suggests that Faustus can disavow it by repenting. And so we have in one awkward document a deed, which sounds final, a contract vague and defective in its terms, and later developments to suggest that nothing is really binding on the parties at all.

Allowing for the passage of centuries since the writing of that document, we still conclude that Faustus and Mephistophilis should have brought in their lawyers.

The present chapter on drafting is addressed to members of the legal profession whose first language is other than English, and to native English speakers who are studying law. The layman, too, may consider it with profit, but to a different end. For him it may emphasize what Chaucer calls "The lyf so short, the craft so longe to lerne."

A Contract Order

In Chapter 3 we dealt with one of the expanding leisure industries in terms of hardware. Our hypothetical case in this chapter deals with software, since the concepts involved in dealing with copyrights and other intangibles are more complex and taxing to the imagination.

Assume an American client known as Trans-Globe Communications, Inc., sends in a contract order along these lines:

> We just got world television rights to this year's top sports event, the Wassail World Match-Play Championship Golf Match held annually in May at Penzance, Cornwall. The rights owners are Flagon Breweries, Ltd., in Liverpool, who make Wassail beer and stout. They have tentative arrangements with Cornwall

Television whereby Cornwall transmits in the UK and sets up world coverage by satellite via the Post Office or Museum, still to be worked out. We get exclusive foreign broadcasting and foreign merchandising rights for £1000 payable to Flagon Breweries on signing. As an exception, Flagon keeps 16-mm film rights for nonprofit exhibition and for television broadcast not before six months following what we arrange ourselves.

We pay Cornwall's facilities charge, recoup in first position, and then split net profits with the brewery. They handle the billing and collection of licensing fees.

As usual, I need a contract yesterday.

After several telephone calls for clarification, the drafting begins. In considering this phase of Contract English we invert the procedure used in the last chapter, setting out the thought process before the text of the agreement, not after it. In doing so, we follow the usual sequence of events that characterizes drafting. When analyzing somebody else's contracts you read first, then reflect. When drafting your own, the reverse is more appropriate.

Instead of questions and answers this time we merely use notes to reflect the draftsman's stream of consciousness. And now, feet on desk, we begin working.

Definitions This contract calls for definitions. Even exclusivity can be defined at the beginning because the brewers retain certain nonprofit film rights as an exception. I could spell that out later on, but it will read more like a story if I define what things mean at the outset and divide up their ownership afterwards. For example, I can define television rights at great length and then have a separate clause saying essentially, "We have them."

That part of it is relatively simple. I can define television rights and net profits by adapting from past models. What really worries me is how to define the golf match itself. Without the widest possible definition, my client has nothing.

What exactly is the Wassail World Match-Play Championship Golf Match? The point is, do we still have the rights if they change the name, or the locale, or the format, or the management? All of that must be protected. I have no intention of losing everything because some Liverpool brewery decides at the last minute to call it the Flagon Golf Pageant or hold it at Baden-Baden. Everyone would know it was still the Wassail World Match-Play Championship in disguise. But would they, if it were actually held in Baden-Baden? I musn't try and carry this too far. Some changes preserve the identity; others destroy it. Surely for example a postponement of the date keeps it the same event. This had better be drawn broadly, however, to protect my client.

Time to begin. I think the brewery people granting the rights should be called "Owner" and my client "Distributor," not some sort of agent who takes instructions and acts as fiduciary. No phone calls; say I am out at a meeting. And now, text:

> AGREEMENT made this ——— day of ————— 19——, by and between Flagon Breweries, Ltd., of 37 Quench Street, Liverpool ("Owner"), and Trans-Globe Communications, Inc., of 500 East 64th Street, New York City, N.Y. ("Distributor").
>
> 1. For the purposes of this agreement the following definitions shall be applicable:
>
> *a*. The Match refers to the Wassail World Match-Play Championship Golf Match scheduled to be held in May, 19——, at Penzance, Cornwall, and includes without limitation the same or any substantially similar event presented under a different name or different management or at a different location or on a rescheduled date provided only that there be some identifiable element of continuity between the Match as altered and any of its predecessor events in past years.

Foreign Television Rights Trans-Globe told me that Cornwall Television keeps UK rights but we have the rest of the world. They also said cigarette commercials are excluded. Theatrical exhibition rights and video cassette rights are reserved as well. Luckily these client afterthoughts came in time for the first draft.

What worries me is that my people have to work out the facilities payment with Cornwall Television. If the price is too high, are we in breach to the brewery? This will have to be handled delicately. Perhaps saying "a charge acceptable to Distributor" gives us enough leeway. Text:

> *b*. "Foreign Television Rights" means, and includes without limitation, the right to arrange, with Cornwall Television or any other company which makes a live television broadcast or telerecording of the Match, for compliance with the requirements of program licensees and governmental authority by introduction of an American commentator and otherwise, and to the same end to edit, translate, dub, and alter the program and cause the insertion or deletion of commercial advertising material except insertion of cigarette commercials; to negotiate with

Cornwall Television or its successor a facilities charge acceptable to Distributor at Distributor's sole discretion for payment by Distributor; and to effect and arrange, perpetually and without limitation anywhere and everywhere throughout the world except the United Kingdom, unlimited television broadcasts and distribution of the program recording the Match fully or in part, in any form or language, and in black and white or color by means of tape, film, or any other device now known or hereafter devised including live origination and satellite coupled with any other similar or dissimilar events or material, and presented as one program or multiple programs, all as designated solely by Distributor. The program may be thus exhibited on "free" network, regional and/or local television either broadcast or by cable or community antenna television or any and all among them but not in theaters where payment is charged for attendance or by video cassette or any form of pay or subscription television, which are excluded from Foreign Television Rights and reserved to Owner together with United Kingdom television rights of every description.

Exclusivity Now to define "exclusively" with the exception of 16 mm. I ought to freeze all the rights Flagon reserves wherever possible, but one thing they will be entitled to is a few minutes of nonexclusivity to show program extracts on the news. The number of minutes can be left blank for Trans-Globe to negotiate. Text:

c. "Exclusive" means that neither Owner nor any other person, firm, or corporation except Distributor may deal in, exploit, grant, or exercise the same or substantially competitive rights except that Owner may, in addition to its United Kingdom rights, distribute throughout the world a 16-mm film of the Match not exceeding ——— minutes in length for private viewing at any time in golf clubs and associations where no payment is made for admission to the viewing, and for television broadcast of such film anywhere commencing on a release date no sooner than six months from the completion of initial telecast everywhere as arranged by Distributor or ——— months from the date of this agreement, whichever is later; and Owner may also at any time arrange the licensing of not more than ——— minutes of the Match anywhere for telecast only on a regularly scheduled national network news program. All other television rights whose use is not partitioned in this definition of "Exclusive," such as pay and theatrical television, will not be granted, exercised, exploited, or otherwise used by either party without the other's advance written permission anywhere except solely in the United Kingdom by Owner as set forth above.

Net Profits Since the brewers handle money collections, I want something elaborate with "directly or indirectly" to prevent any concealment. Be sure to bring in that the Americans recoup facilities charges before profits are split up, and they deduct all of the other costs and commissions too. No, I see a file note of my fifth telephone conversation with this client, where they said they agreed to no other deductions except profit shares payable to third parties. This is awful. Possibly next time they may do better. Text:

> *d.* "Net Profits" shall mean and include all licensing fees and other monies received directly or indirectly by Owner anywhere from and attributable to the exercise by Distributor of its rights in and to the program recording the Match less only and subject to the deduction of the facilities charge paid or payable to BBC or its successor for United Kingdom telecast (which Distributor shall first recoup) and less and subject to the deduction of any segment of Distributor's share of Net Profits assigned by Distributor to any third party in connection with its arrangements for exploitation and distribution of the program anywhere, but subject to a different formula in defining Net Profits in connection with Foreign Merchandising Rights as set forth below.

Foreign Merchandising Rights Here we can get a better definition of net profits, which is why the net profits definition in paragraph *d* points out at the end that merchandising will be different. Now I have a new problem.

What about the names and likenesses of players in the match? The client expects to make clothing and other merchandise exploiting these assets. Who clears the rights? Flagon must do it. Let me try running it in with the title and other material which the brewery delivers. If they object, we can work something out later on: Text:

> *e.* "Foreign Merchandising Rights" means and includes the right to arrange, effect manufacture of, sell, and distribute throughout the world except the United Kingdom on terms solely of Distributor's designation the physical replicas of all or any segment of the Match including without limitation players participating in the Match, the name of the Match and the names of participant players, the program title, any phrase or other distinctive symbol used in the Match or in the program, and other material connected with or arising out of the program, for reproduction or use in connection with articles of clothing, athletic equipment, dolls, figurines, books, gramophone records, and other devices which can be made use of in commercial tie-ins, but in no event as a specific endorsement of any product or service. Net Profits from Foreign Merchandising Rights shall be computed after deduction and recoupment of all distribution costs and fees, commissions, and profit shares payable by Distributor to any third party.

The Grant Now we reap the harvest of all these elaborate definitions. All that remains to be said is that we get what was defined. I wish the £1000 payment were some sort of advance recoupable before profits are divided, but Trans-Globe gave it away. Our sixth telephone conversation made that all too clear. Text:

2. For consideration in the sum of £1000 (One thousand pounds), receipt of which Owner hereby acknowledges, and for other valuable but contingent consideration set forth below, Owner hereby grants, assigns, transfers, and sets over irrevocably to Distributor the Exclusive Foreign Television Rights and Exclusive Foreign Merchandising Rights in and to the Match.

Accountings This ought to be fairly simple. The one thing to prevent is Flagon's carrying losses from broadcasting against merchandising, or vice versa. "No cross-collateralization" is the term I want. Keep the operations separate. Text:

3. The parties will divide equally between them Net Profits from Foreign Television Rights and Foreign Merchandising Rights, 50% to Distributor and 50% to Owner, with no cross-collateralization between this and any other transaction that may be entered into between the parties to this agreement or between either party and any third party. Owner will be responsible for billing and collections and Distributor will in its licensing arrangements with third parties designate Owner as the payee. Owner will keep separate accurate books and records of all transactions hereunder which may be inspected by Distributor at any time during reasonable business hours upon prior written notice of —————. Owner will furnish Distributor with copies of all accountings received by Owner, and in any event with certified accountings every —months from the date of this agreement, and will immediately upon receipt pay over to Distributor whatever segment of Net Profits belongs and is payable to Distributor as set forth above. Net Profits from Foreign Merchandising Rights will be similarly but separately accounted for. Owner will maintain separate bank accounts for proceeds from exploitation of Distributor's rights hereunder.

Reserved Rights Apparently we don't share in British proceeds from reserved rights. This ought to be said, even if it helps the other side. Text:

4. Distributor shall not be entitled to any share of Net Profits attributable solely to Owner's exploitation of its reserved United Kingdom rights.

Billing Credit What if the brewery has arrangements with its own people about putting their names on the screen? We may inadvertently be in breach to third parties if we fail to adhere to that. Since I don't know what these obligations are, the brewers ought to say that they will tell us.

Obviously Trans-Globe wants its name on the screen too. So may Flagon of Liverpool. The best thing is to mention the subject and let them decide mutually how each name is to appear. In a way this is an agreement to agree, but I can provide that both will behave "reasonably."

What if the network refuses to broadcast the name credits in the approved form? "Subject to" comes to the rescue. Text:

> 5. Owner and Distributor each will be entitled to appropriate billing credit on the program(s) in a form reasonably approved by the other, and subject to any applicable rules and regulations imposed by program licensees. Owner will disclose to Distributor any contractual billing requirements imposed upon Owner by third parties.

Disavowals I worry about implied promises by Trans-Globe. Suppose we do our best but there still are no net profits? And what if the facilities charge is too high, even though I took care of this in paragraph 1*b*? Worst of all, what happens if something horrible ruins the entire match? Trans-Globe requires protection against all of this, and even against a tournament made up suddenly of fifth-rate players. If something goes wrong, we have nothing to sell. How can we word this with dignity? Text:

> 6. Distributor will use reasonable efforts to distribute the program but cannot give any assurance that there will in fact be Net Profits. Distributor will not be required to enter into facilities arrangements with Cornwall Television or its successor or to undertake or seek any other commitment if the facilities charge by Cornwall Television or its successor proves unacceptable to Distributor or if the program value of the Match is substantially diminished by force majeure or by diminution in the quality of the play or players or by scandal.

Insurance The client mentioned a standard insurance policy carried by American broadcasters. It covers privacy violations and related risks. Perhaps the brewery might like to pay the premiums. Text:

> 7. At its own cost Owner will include Distributor and Distributor's program licensees in a broadcaster's liability errors and omissions

insurance policy with coverage of at least $1 million in connection with Distributor's exercise of its rights hereunder.

Copyrights and Trademarks It does us no good if our rights fall into the public domain so that others can share them. The brewery ought to prevent that and put us in a position to sue others if they won't.

Something else haunts me a little: the possibility that Trans-Globe may invent some original format device which it might need for other events of this kind. Who owns that? The possibility merits a separate paragraph further along in the contract. Just now I want to be sure that the Liverpool people don't lose everything for all of us. Text:

8. At its own cost Owner will secure and maintain throughout the world, wherever such protection is available by local law or by international convention, copyright, trademark, and service mark protection including registration in and to the program recording the Match and all its component elements susceptible of exploitation by merchandising and other rights forming part of the grant hereunder. Owner irrevocably designates Distributor in the maximum degree possible under local laws everywhere except the United Kingdom as the appropriate plaintiff authorized to bring legal and equitable actions in Owner's stead for protection of the rights referred to in this paragraph, and at Owner's cost, if Owner declines to undertake the appropriate action.

Separate Agreement Now a complex point. Flagon has some kind of agreement with Cornwall Television. For all we know, they gave Cornwall some rights that conflict with our own. They may have given them overseas distribution rights even though it would be a breach of our own exclusivity abroad. Or they may have done something less basic but still awkward, such as agreeing that no American commentary will be substituted for the British sound track. We don't know what they've done. Perhaps their financial arrangements are none of our affair, but the rest of it needs disclosure. The time for it is now. Let me draft in terms of disclosure on signing, but we won't actually sign until we see their contract with Cornwall. Text:

9. Simultaneously with entering into this agreement with Distributor, Owner will disclose to Distributor all those provisions of its agreement with Cornwall Television or its successor which set forth the scope of the rights granted and reserved, and of the conditions concerning production of the program(s) except monies payable to Owner.

Options We need some sort of hold on the golf match for future years. There seems no reason, in fact, to confine it to this particular sports event. What if the brewery people control a steeplechase or future tennis championships? And if we drop one of them, must we lose the others? I think we had better try for the brass ring on this one. Text:

> 10. Owner hereby grants to Distributor a series of consecutive exclusive and irrevocable options, to be exercised in each instance if Distributor elects to exercise the applicable option, by the furnishing of written notice to Owner no later than ——— days before the scheduled commencement of Match play, to acquire Exclusive Foreign Television Rights and Exclusive Foreign Merchandising Rights in and to the Match for the next years, i.e. through and including 19——, all upon the same terms and conditions as those governing the present transaction. Throughout the same time period Distributor shall have and Owner hereby grants to Distributor a series of like options to acquire Exclusive Foreign Television Rights and Exclusive Foreign Merchandising Rights in and to all other sports events and athletic contests in which Owner controls either right or both such rights in any country, with the understanding that Distributor may decline to exercise any one or more such options without waiving its rights to exercise any and all remaining options.

Residuals Flagon may have arrangements with participating athletes for extra "residual" payments if the program recording is shown again, or even once. Furthermore I still worry about consents to the use of their names and performances. All of these obligations belong with Liverpool. Text:

> 11. In connection with the Match and any other event for the rights to which Distributor exercises an option hereunder, and as between the parties, Owner will be solely responsible for the payment of residual fees and all other monies to participants in the applicable contest, and for securing in a mutually acceptable form of release, and delivering to Distributor, appropriate and effective signed privacy waivers and other consents by everyone concerned.

Assignment We need assignment rights to sell the Match overseas. Flagon may want to use a subsidiary for reasons of its own. Fair enough, as long as each of us remains ultimately responsible. Text:

> 12. At any time and from time to time either party may assign its rights hereunder fully or in part to anyone or pledge, mortgage, or

hypothecate such rights without restriction provided, however, that the assignor shall remain liable for performance of this agreement if its assignee defaults.

Warranties Get some bristling warranties from the brewery to make sure they have what they propose granting. Most of it can be standard, but injecting a warranty about their arrangement with Cornwall is a good move. Provide that extracts from that contract and anything replacing it be annexed here and now. Text:

13. Owner hereby makes the following warranties and representations concerning the Match and any other event which this agreement encompasses to Distributor for the benefit of Distributor and Distributor's assignees and licensees:

a. that Owner has the right to enter into this agreement without encumbrance and to grant all the exclusive rights herein granted;

b. that all program material respecting the Match including without limitation the title, and any incidental literary, musical or other material presented and furnished in connection with the Match, is free of unlawful matter and encumbrance, except with respect to any material inserted by Distributor;

c. that Owner has secured and can lawfully and will assign to Distributor all releases and clearances necessary for Distributor's exercise of its Foreign Television Rights and Foreign Merchandising Rights hereunder at no cost to Distributor;

d. that Owner has complied with the rules and regulations of any union having jurisdiction and will be solely responsible for any payments required in connection with such compliance and for any and all payments required to be made to participating contestants for consenting to the exercise of the Foreign Television Rights and Foreign Merchandising Rights granted herein;

e. that Owner knows of no outstanding claim or legal action adverse to the grant of rights hereunder or relating to the Match in any way;

f. that Owner will not undertake or permit exercise by anyone anywhere of its reserved rights except under any applicable conditions set forth above;

g. that Owner at no cost to Distributor has secured and will maintain effective copyright, trademark, and service mark protection, wherever such protection is available, of all elements constituting the subject matter of the rights grant hereunder;

h. that the annexed extracts from Owner's agreement dated ——————— with Cornwall Television concerning the Match constitute and will continue throughout the term hereof to constitute all of the listed terms and provisions applicable to prospective Cornwall

Television telecast of the Match, and that similar extracts from agreements with Cornwall's successor, if any, will be disclosed and will be consistent with and subject to the terms of the present agreement between Owner and Distributor;

i. that to the best of Owner's knowledge there is not and will not be any unlawful or irregular practice in the playing of the Match or in its outcome.

Owner will indemnify and hold harmless Distributor and Distributor's directors, officers, agents, assignees, and licensees from, against, and with respect to any and all claims, losses, damages, expenses (including reasonable counsel fees), and other liabilities arising out of or in connection with Owner's breach of any warranty or representation hereunder. Distributor will similarly indemnify Owner in respect of any program material interpolated by Distributor.

Subdistributors Trans-Globe may need to use local agents in any number of countries and split its share. Possibly the right to assign covers this, but we had better make sure. Text:

14. Distributor may at any time and from time to time appoint agents, subdistributors, and other deputies anywhere except in the United Kingdom to assist in the promotion of its rights hereunder without, however, affecting the definition of Net Profits set forth earlier in this agreement.

Independent Contractors Usually we have a provision limiting how much "we and they" are in business together. Too close a relationship can be dangerous. Text:

15. Nothing in this agreement is designed to create a joint venture, partnership, agency, or taxable entity between the parties, or any right to pledge the other's credit, it being understood that Owner and Distributor are independent contractors vis-à-vis one another.

Overages Still nagging at me is the possibility that one side's costs will go over budget and be imposed on the other. Text:

16. As between the parties, and subject to the definition of Net Profits set forth above, Owner is solely responsible for all costs including unanticipated overages in connection with the Match and its television broadcast in the United Kingdom, and Distributor is responsible for all costs including unanticipated overages in distributing the program(s) outside the United Kingdom, except as varied elsewhere in this agreement.

Delivery None of this is much use if the program recording is undelivered or inadequate. When it comes to the satellite arrangements, the specifics are too technical for me. The best thing is to use general language putting all of that burden on the others. "Appropriate" is a good word, and Trans-Globe's "requirements" even better. Nothing but acts of God can excuse Flagon from arranging the overseas signal. Text:

> 17. Owner agrees and will ensure that the telerecorded program(s) of the Match will be promptly delivered to Distributor at no cost to Distributor in a form and of a quality sufficient to meet professional United States and other national television network standards for television broadcasting. In any arrangements with Cornwall Television or its successor, Owner will require delivery to Distributor of ——— telerecordings of the program(s) and Distributor will bear no responsibility for delivery or transportation charges within a radius of——— from the metropolitan area of London. Owner will at no cost to Distributor similarly ensure the availability of appropriate satellite facilities for transmission live or on video tape or a combination of both as required by Distributor in connection with its program format, subject only to force majeure and the unavailability of such satellite facilities for reasons other than cost.

Injunction What if the brewery commits breach? Money damages are inadequate if they grant the same rights to somebody else. We need an injunction, which might be available under American law if the rights are unique. And unique they most certainly are. It will be more diplomatic and nearly as strong to say "unique" without "injunction." Besides, we can't tell a future court what relief to provide. Text:

> 18. Owner acknowledges that the Match and the rights granted in this agreement are unique.

Mergers It suddenly occurs to me that the match may become part of some bigger series run by an association. We ought to have the rights to use the collective name. Text:

> 19. If and to the degree the Match is or becomes connected with a league or association in the field of professional athletics, or if and to any extent Owner does so, the name and other identifying symbols of the larger group will be included in the grant of rights to Distributor and Owner will be responsible for securing any necessary written consents and permissions in order to give effect to the provisions of this paragraph.

Related Activities Can the brewery criticize us for taking on similar events for others? Not very likely, but it may be useful to be sure of it. And this is the best place for keeping our format material without disturbing their own. Text:

> 20. Distributor reserves the right at any time to act on its own account and for others in distributing similar programs and exploiting similar rights in other sports events, and Distributor reserves the exclusive ownership of any and all original program material, including text, commentary, and format, and of identifying devices and all other incorporeal property acquired, devised, or used by Distributor in connection with the exercise of its rights granted hereunder, except for any such material furnished by Owner specifically identifying the Match itself, which material nevertheless forms part of the grant and is subject to the terms and provisions set forth earlier in this agreement.

Timing What if Trans-Globe's American sale depends on transmission no later than in the UK? And what if British golf caps are exported to Germany before we get there with our own? Very little can be done, but have Flagon "consult and cooperate." Text:

> 21. For the purpose of enabling Distributor to secure licensing agreements, Owner will consult and cooperate with Distributor concerning priorities of initial television broadcast in the United Kingdom and foreign markets and concerning United Kingdom export of British merchandising articles abroad.

Subsidiary Rights Morbid afterthought: what if one of the famous golfers writes something valuable which is honestly connected with the match itself? If this is sold outside the UK, we ought to share. Text:

> 22. Owner's share of any proceeds outside the United Kingdom derived from the turning to account by contestants of memoirs or other properties based on or engendered by the Match, in any medium not coming within the definitions of rights granted to Distributor, will be divisible as Net Profits.

Signing Off Conclude with the usual pleasantries but say nothing about whose law governs until we see how negotiations proceed. With these international transactions we may want to give this point some thought and research. There may be a convention or treaty on satellite broadcasting. Without one, country X may pirate the contest out of space. Just for now the usual signatures are enough. Text:

23. All notices provided for in this agreement shall be addressed to the recipient party at the address set forth above, or to a different address previously designated by the applicable party in writing, and shall be deemed sufficient when so deposited in the mail, postage prepaid, or delivered so addressed to a telegraph or cable company toll prepaid.

24. This constitutes the full agreement between the parties and can be amended only in writing.

Trans-Globe Communications, Inc.	Flagon Breweries, Ltd.
by:	by:

Summary

We have now sampled a draftsman's thought process, including his dismay at aspects of the transaction itself. A good contract can do little to improve a bad deal. In our case of the satellite, for example, the Distributor should be able to deduct distribution fees and certain costs before sharing profits with the Owner. Since the contrary has been agreed to, however, all the draftsman can do is follow instructions.

In articulating his thought process, we have emphasized concepts more than his final choice of words. The words themselves appear immediately after the concepts engendering them. Listing all of the rejected phrases would fill up volumes.

Nevertheless the final text is what counts, and it is worth mulling over. Undoubtedly there are better ways of saying many of the same things; often the adversary's lawyer invents them. Perhaps it will be fair to suggest that the quoted passages are representative of decent Contract English. The choice of an international television contract as a showcase was deliberate; very little else is as up to the minute or as likely to stretch the imagination so painfully. One of the main problems we considered was defining the event itself. What if it moved to the Black Forest or turned up in September instead of May? Few other agreements create such extraordinary dilemmas.

And few other languages possess the richness to deal with them.

CHAPTER FIVE

The Art of Compromise

Whoever drafts a contract must expect that the other side will raise objections to it and require changes. It may not be overly cynical to suggest that the absence of objections ought to put the draftsman on guard; something may have been left out that the adversary is happy to keep buried. The normal course of events, however, involves contest, and the usual outcome of contest is compromise.

Aesopian Phrases

At this point we confront one of the most subtle and deceptive riddles of all. When is verbiage only a word or phrase, and when is it something more? The distinction is vital; we touched on it in an earlier chapter, but in settling disputes it looms larger still and requires refinement.

There is a minor fashion nowadays to call certain language "Aesopian," suggesting that it has hidden meaning, as fables do. Phrases such as "imperialistic elements," "certain minorities," even "those who disagree" may be understood by the reader or listener without being made more specific. Close analysis discloses two elements in this kind of phrasing, namely characterization and disguise.

Characterization is putting labels on things frequently better off without them. "Pandora Jenks was typical county stock" goes well enough in a bad novel, but further description of her as "dolichocephalic" is unhelpful because it adds nothing except irrelevance; her head structure will be uninteresting to the majority of readers.

Disguise adds an element of deception. Not all deception is deliberate or malevolent, but the mask nevertheless must be plucked off and true identification achieved.

The relevance of these reflections can be demonstrated by the simplest sort of example. A seller acting completely in good faith might put this phrase into a contract: "The Seller makes absolutely no warranties or representations concerning title, except that Exhibit I annexed is a true and accurate copy of the assignment to the Seller by the previous owner, and the Buyer acquires the Seller's rights (if any) on a quitclaim basis without express or implied assurances of any kind whatsoever." Something is wrong here. On second glance (even on first glance if you are feeling particularly keen) the crack in the wall appears. To say, "without express or implied assurances of any kind whatsoever" negates and takes away the one assurance that was in fact grudgingly given—that Exhibit I is a true copy. Characterization and disguise join in destroying the logic of the clause in question. "There are no animals in the barn except mice" cannot support the addendum, "no living creatures whatever."

More than inconsistency is involved. In these examples the illogical thought appears in words different from the original statement. Concepts are mixed up and the error comes on masked.

Compromising disputed points requires the ability to penetrate disguise and decipher hidden meanings. All too often we bemuse ourselves with words, just as our ancestors relied on runes and spells to promote desired events.

Words can work magic, but only if the concepts they embody make sense. At least this is true with contracts; whether words can cure horses and make crops grow is a separate subject.

The Need for Language Formulas

The alteration of draft language sharpens the distinction between words and concepts. It will be one thing to request changes in phraseology because the wording seems unclear, or even for more subjective reasons such as dislike of "eschew" instead of "forgo." It will be quite another thing, however, to change what is actually meant to happen as the parties perform their contract. The art of compromise involves both, and learning to distinguish one from the other is apprenticeship in the art, just as imagination is the ingredient for its mastery.

Up to now we have been considering the classic course of business negotiations. After preliminary chapters on law and language, there were samples of probing, fencing, and position-taking as people tiptoed (if they did things properly) into commitments. Then came the analysis of written proposals and eventually the composition of drafts. Step by step we came closer to making contracts in English, until we reached the present stage, when the draft is objected to and only compromise can unlock the impasse.

This is the final stage in the usual course of negotiation. Either solutions are found or the whole transaction is called off. Somewhere soon there is going to be a need for compromise "formulas." As these are invented, it will be necessary to distinguish between changes in the wording and changes in the transaction itself.

The invention of formulas is best illustrated by picking up where Chapter 4 left off. Let us reconsider the proposed television contract, with a new element introduced for the purpose of tracing the evolution of compromise. We are going to deal with rather a larger number of proposed formulas than might ordinarily be the case in actual commerce, where time presses and nerves weaken. The following outline, however, is made artificially thorough so as to illustrate how many ways there are of going at the same thing. At least our protagonists have lots of energy, and we can pretend that they have lots of time as well.

In the television example an American company called Trans-Globe Communications busied itself getting the rights to the Wassail World Match-Play Championship Golf Match from Flagon Breweries in Liverpool, coordinating its rights with the UK broadcaster, Cornwall Television. We now add a new fact that creates opportunity, but it creates difficulty as well.

The new fact is that a German association of sausage makers offers to pay generously for the right to put up placards saying "German Sausage Is Best" at various points on the golf course at Penzance where they will be seen by the television audience. It all seems very attractive and simple. Flagon Breweries agrees that the Americans can work out the arrangements with Germany, dividing the proceeds between them subject to whatever Cornwall Television requires for its role in the good deed. Trans-Globe is elected to deal with Cornwall.

The American acting in this matter is an ex-lawyer turned producer named M. Cornwall Television is represented by X, its head of sports programming. Now M is keen on having everything go his own way, and X is famous for having her way in everything, so a brisk dialogue is inevitable.

A First Formula M is aware that the advertising agency acting for the Germans will require some sort of assurance that their placards will be prominently visible to home viewers via television, not merely to spectators physically present at Penzance. Without that, the Germans never would contract to pay for the placards, and their agency has already been given oral assurance that everything can be arranged. ("Has been arranged" rather than "can be arranged" is more likely to have been promised in the world as it is, but Trans-Globe is famous for impeccable behavior.) M writes as follows:

> Dear X:
>
> As you know, we have an agreement with Flagon Breweries giving us certain rights to the Wassail Match for this and subsequent years. We understand that you are broadcasting this event for the UK.
>
> A West German client has approached the Flagon people and ourselves, who act for Flagon in this matter, with an offer for posting several placards reading "German Sausage Is Best" where they will do the most good in terms of the television viewing audience. We have not yet worked out the exact placements, but we would like your written confirmation that no problems exist so that your contract with Flagon can be amended accordingly.
>
> In addition it will be necessary, for obvious reasons, to phrase this in language that puts an affirmative obligation on your camera crew and other technicians to show this advertising to best advantage. I suggest language such as "Cornwall, subject only to acts of God and network preemption for national emergency, will assure prominent and continuing visibility to any number of signs, billboards, and placards not in excess of ——— reading 'German Sausage Is Best' at the situs of the Wassail Match so that all such signs, billboards, and placards, in whatever sizes and placements the Rights Owners designate, will

be captured on camera together with the Match itself and transmitted to home audiences and other spectators no less prominently than the Match itself."

I look forward to your confirmation so that our lawyers can draw up the amendment.

X replies:

Dear M:

Thank you for your letter of September 2 last. Unfortunately this company cannot accommodate you in respect of the proposed advertising at the Match. You must be aware that we are required under our charter to retain absolute control over what is transmitted for broadcast. Any assurance such as you propose would be in violation of the charter and of our policy as well.

It is true that the name "Flagon Breweries" appeared in past years at the Match, but this was left up to our discretion and never guaranteed.

I might consider, "Placards advertising German sausage and permanently fixed at the situs of the Match may be transmitted subject to clearance by Cornwall's General Solicitor," but nothing more.

Even that much could be reflected only in a letter of intent, not a contract amendment.

A Second Formula M replies:

Dear X:

Thank you for your letter of September 7. You in turn surely must realize that your suggestion would be unacceptable in terms of our German advertiser. Sponsors make payment only for value received.

I appreciate your policy and charter problems that made guarantees impossible. Here is an alternative that might be acceptable:

"Cornwall is fully aware that the Rights Owners have entered into contractual commitments with an advertiser for television coverage of its placards at the Match situs, reading 'German Sausage Is Best.' Cornwall agrees, and will instruct its director, camera crew, and other technicians not to avoid, minimize, or limit reasonable coverage of such placards in its transmission or in edited recordings thereof."

I think that solves our little problem. This way you avoid

guaranteeing anything affirmatively, and I look forward to your quick confirmation that everything is agreed.

X shows her annoyance in replying:

> Your revised formula says the same thing, only negatively. I can only repeat that there is no way in which this company will limit its complete control of program content.

A Third Formula M writes:

> I disagree that a negative undertaking is the same thing. May I suggest that we deal with this problem in a practical way, keeping in mind that I am only trying to avoid breach of our obligations to the Germans and not to score points against you or your company.
>
> My idea now is simply to recite, "Cornwall is aware of the Rights Owners' obligations to a third party under an agreement dated ———, a copy of which is annexed hereto as Exhibit I, and Cornwall will not knowingly do or authorize the commission or omission of any act that would reasonably tend to put the rights owners in breach of Exhibit I."
>
> Will that do it?

X in reply:

> Your latest suggestion is unacceptable. Once again you seem to be putting the same thought in different words. Obviously your contract with the Germans would limit our control by assuring them of things that we ourselves would undertake to make good if we went along with it.
>
> I have discussed this with our General Solicitor, who sees no reason to modify anything I have said previously.

A Fourth Formula M:

> What about keeping it vague, as you suggest, with language of this sort that never mentions German sausage:
>
> "Cornwall agrees to transmit and record the Match and the surroundings, including spectators, as in past years."
>
> After all, you did well enough with the Flagon signs and I am willing to use that as a yardstick. Also there would be spectators at the Germans' placards so the whole thing could be taken care of without even mentioning advertisements. Surely that violates no policy or charter.

And the inevitable reply:

> Perhaps I am not making myself clear. We will not in any way limit our control, even by vague reference to what happened with somebody else at a different time. It all comes down to the same thing, as you surely appreciate. I think it would be best to abandon discussion of this matter.

A Fifth Formula At this point, M dictates but discards the following letter:

> Madam:
>
> You have said No to me once too often. I suggest that your zeal for Virtue has overtaken your good judgment utterly; a touch of the Flexible is not necessarily Weakness, nor Compassion the hallmark of Corruption. I consider you, Madam, and your colleagues as well to be thoroughly disagreeable.

Instead this letter issues:

> I have your reply, which reached me just before the Christmas holidays. In the spirit of that season, I suggest that Cornwall should receive ten percent (10%) of whatever my company receives as its share of the German advertising revenue. What I ask in return will be any of the formulas I have previously suggested, or something to that effect.

X's reply follows:

> This company's charter, together with policy considerations, precludes sharing in the proceeds from advertising. To save time, I am asking you not to start phrasing the same idea in different ways, such as offering a consultancy fee measured by sponsorship proceeds or by the number of German sausages sold in England. Thank you anyhow for the offer.

At this stage a pause is called for, because the direction has changed. M's initial four formulas did, more or less, say the same thing. One said it affirmatively, another negatively by precluding the opposite; the last two brought in standards from outside, first a contract and then the physical surroundings and past practice, all to the same end. X saw that each of these formulas limited her control.

In the fifth formula, however, M injects something which is substantively new. Offering to pay for what he wants is more than a new way of saying the same thing. Admittedly he falls back on the original ideas in exchange, but any negotiator would recognize that he was really inviting new formulas from the other side. Offering to share proceeds was intended to open any number of new doors. That they remained closed did not deter him.

A Sixth Formula

Dear X:

We are now into the New Year, and the German contract is slipping away from me. Since you keep returning to charter and policy considerations, I am going to propose language that makes due allowance for both:

"Cornwall and the Rights Owners will, by mutual agreement within three days from the signing hereof, appoint an arbitrator who shall be a distinguished member of the Bar familiar with the laws of England relating to television broadcasting and who shall be furnished by Cornwall with confidential copies of its charter and policy regulations concerning advertising. The said arbitrator shall promptly render a written opinion concerning the degree of and rules concerning advertising permitted thereunder, which opinion shall be binding on the parties, with the understanding that Cornwall will implement promptly whatever measures the opinion recommends or accepts as not prohibited by charter or policy considerations."

I think you must agree that my latest proposal is fair.

X's reply:

Dear M:

No.

A Seventh Formula M writes:

I see now that I was mistaken in suggesting profit sharing or arbitration. Now indulge me in one last try. You say that my first four formulas come down to the same thing put a little differently, which may be true. My fifth is unacceptable on different grounds, although at least you recognize that I am saying something different. Similarly with the sixth, where I assume you choose to interpret your own charter and policy without outside help. I suggest a seventh, which is my last attempt. It most certainly is not a rewording of anything that went before, and while money is involved there is nothing about sharing in advertising proceeds. There are no arbitrators, even though an outside standard is used. In fact, I am making a completely new proposal.

My proposal is based on the principle of the carrot and the stick. One acts as a reward, the other as punishment. It goes on the assumption that effective camera coverage in one year will encourage the Germans to advertise the year after, while bad coverage will drive them and other sponsors away.

As you may have gathered, I am prepared to offer you options on the Match for three more seasons. I cleared this with Flagon, and they are willing to go along, but solely on condition that you accept our formula for advertising. Leaving the percentages blank, it would go something like this:

"Cornwall is aware that the Rights Owners invite sponsorship by advertisers whose signs and placards at the course are placed so as to be clearly visible to the television audience and that the Rights Owners retain all of the proceeds from such advertising. In view of its possible additional revenues therefrom, the Rights Owners agree that in any and each year under this agreement in which its gross receipts collected solely as the result of and attributable to such advertising at the Match shall exceed the sum of £——— and shall also exceed the aggregate of such advertising revenues collected during the directly preceding year, then X% of the difference between such collections and the directly preceding year's collections shall be credited against the otherwise applicable UK transmission price for the next succeeding year specified in paragraph ——, in reduction thereof. To the contrary effect if in any contract year hereunder the Rights Owners' advertising collections drop below £——— or below the aggregate of such collections during the directly preceding year, then the UK transmission price for the next succeeding year shall be increased, over and beyond and in addition to any increase provided in paragraph —— hereof, by —— % of the amount by which such collections shall have fallen short of £——— or of collections during the directly preceding year, whichever is the greater."

We at Trans-Globe are aware that this accomplishes indirectly what we have tried to accomplish in a more direct way. I deny in advance, however, that it divests you of program control under a disguised verbal formula. On the contrary, it leaves control where it apparently belongs: with you. I deny in advance, too, that it constitutes indirect payment of sponsorship revenues. Your rewards do correlate with these revenues, but for a different year. I deny in advance, finally, that somebody else's judg-

> ment would govern your charter and policy rules. Only the marketplace would serve as judge, and only in judgment of how much more or less you paid for the Match in later years, not of your regulations.
>
> I think that you, as a broadcaster, will recognize something of value in this final proposal. Three more years under option, and a price discount if your people play fair.
>
> Please telex reply, as the Germans are ready to walk out.

Telex reply from X:

> Interested in your proposal for option years. Advertising formula not acceptable but am coming to New York next week and suggest meeting to explore alternatives. Regards. X.

An Ironic Conclusion

Thus ends our anatomy of compromise. One formula follows another, with nearly all of the concessions in this case coming from one side. On closer inspection, the concessions are more apparent than real, so that it may be more accurate to say that nearly all of the initiative comes from one side. However that may be, this extended exercise repays study. It illustrates flailing at the central target, then changing direction suddenly and trying to go round by the side. At first everything is all words, then finally there are several new thoughts. Halfway through, the one with more to gain from successful dialogue begins showing some imagination.

And how does the story end? It can end any number of ways, not all of them neat and tidy. The optimist will have X and M work out a tight little contract in New York, X getting two option years instead of three and M getting some written pledge to aim the cameras "in good faith and with awareness of but no obligation to protect advertising commitments." The Germans will be satisfied and export more sausage.

The pessimist envisions a different outcome. M and X practically come to blows but decide at the last minute to risk the advertising with no contract between them. The Germans complain of inadequate coverage and threaten litigation. Cornwall's camera director swears that the placards were shown better than the golf champions. Trans-Globe and Flagon lose the German account, and M gets food poisoning from some of the sausages.

Sooner or later all of the alternative endings are played out. Each production, however, has a different author and your own skill is what shapes the outcome.

A Clean-cut Result

In the foregoing example, nothing really definitive or tangible emerged as the end product. This is so frequently the case that to suggest otherwise would mislead, especially in a chapter on compromise. The essence of compromise is really little more than to realize that everybody is unhappy but can live with concessions made to keep peace. A clean kill is the exception.

Not every compromise, however, involves as much thrashing about with so little to show for it as the case of M versus X above. That elaborate a dispute over one point is useful as a great plum pudding of an example, with everything in it, but not so easily digested. It creates a yearning for something simpler, and so we conclude with another example, only with less in it and with a signed document as the conclusion.

"Licensee will use best efforts to sell Licensor's products within the territory." That simple clause appears in the draft of a proposed licensing agreement. The Licensee, however, finds it a little claustrophobic. The following correspondence ensues, illustrating among other things how one point suggests another until you have several dilemmas instead of one requiring solution.

The Dangers of Pledging One's Best The Licensee writes:

> I cannot accept the clause "Licensee will use best efforts to sell Licensor's products within the territory." Obviously we are going to do our best, especially since the contract puts us on a commission basis, but I don't know what "best efforts" are and my colleagues and I feel you should take us on good faith. Our reputation in the field is well established.

The Licensor replies:

> The "best efforts" clause is in all of our contracts. In contracts with English licensees we call it "best endeavors." Please don't assume that it holds you to any particular guaranteed sales figure, although we would certainly want the right to get out of it if figures were too low in a particular year.

Licensee:

What do you mean by "get out of it if figures were too low in a particular year"? This is a new point.

Licensor:

Please refer to our Standard Terms and Conditions sent under separate cover. The contract incorporates these conditions as with all our licenses. We see no reason why any of this should impose any hardship since you will only be handling our line anyway.

Licensee:

Once again you seem to be raising a new point. Our lawyers have had a look at the Standard Terms and Conditions, and they advise us that we are prohibited only from dealing in competitive products in the same category, all as explicitly listed. We are not precluded from handling other lines at all, and if your interpretation is different, that would be all the more reason to avoid "best efforts." We agree, however, that you can terminate if minimum sales in the first year are less than $500,000 in the aggregate.

The Licensor replies:

I'm glad we have resolved the cutoff figure. On the other point, exclusivity, I agree that you can sell anything for other people as long as it isn't listed in the Standard Terms and Conditions section on preclusions.

Now that these other points are worked out, you can see that "best efforts" is harmless. I hope the contract is ready for signature next week.

The Search for Alternatives The additional points that arose were suggested by one vapid phrase. They were closely related to "best efforts" in that they implemented its vague requirements. Just what is involved in doing one's best? Does it mean giving up everything else in the same area? Does it require abandonment of the main relationship itself if initial results are disappointing? These are some of the consequences that might flow from accepting imposed standards of behavior. Each of them is best dealt with in a separate provision to make sensible contracts.

Assume, however, that these various side points have been worked out. The parties are left with "Licensee will use best efforts to sell Licensor's products within the territory." The periphery is adjusted, but not the core. After certain adventures, we are back to square one.

The Licensee writes:

> My daughter is in her last year at Harvard, where she is consistently top of the class in English. She has suggested the following list of phrases to replace "best efforts" and impose somewhat lesser requirements on my company:
>
> 1. Will make efforts (no adjective characterizing the efforts)
> 2. Efforts consonant with normal practice
> 3. Bona fide efforts
> 4. Fair efforts
> 5. Active efforts
> 6. Workmanlike efforts
> 7. Efforts no lesser than with other accounts
> 8. Substantial efforts
> 9. Suitable efforts with no implied guarantees of success
> 10. Efforts appropriate in the circumstances
> 11. Its standard efforts
> 12. Reasonable efforts
>
> I feel sure that something in this list will suit you.

The Licensor replies:

> My lawyers advise me that "reasonable efforts" will be acceptable. Our deal is set.

What "reasonable" means may be open to dispute, but it solves this case.

A Final Example

We arrive now at the end of a long journey through shifting scenes and many hazards. The subject of the tour was The Making of a Contract. In a book concerned chiefly with business contracts, we have had to keep to the main road through industrial areas; but we miss out on the byways and a touch of the countryside. This rigorous chapter, accordingly, concludes with a contract by a master of prose. In a final example, we consider the Art of Compromise in different terms. Even prime ministers have coffee breaks.

Our example is the contract of marriage. You may find it wanting in the true spirit of compromise, but the phrasing is unexcelled as a classic of Contract English. Here is part of Act IV, Scene 5 from Congreve's *The Way of the World,* in which Mrs. Millamant and Mirabell become engaged, subject to certain conditions:

MILLA: Ah, don't be impertinent–My dear liberty, shall I leave thee? My faithful solitude, my darling contemplation, must I bid you then adieu? Ay-h adieu – my morning thoughts, agreeable wakings, indolent slumbers, all ye douceurs, ye sommeils du matin, adieu – I can't do it, 'tis more than impossible. – Positively, Mirabell, I'll lie a-bed in a morning as long as I please.

MIRA: Then I'll get up in a morning as early as I please.

MILLA: Ah! Idle creature, get up when you will–And d'ye hear, I won't be called names after I'm married; positively I won't be call'd names.

MIRA: Names!

MILLA: Ay, as wife, spouse, my dear, joy, jewel, love, sweetheart, and the rest of that nauseous cant, in which men and their wives are so fulsomely familiar, – I shall never bear that. – Good Mirabell, don't let us be familiar or fond, nor kiss before folks, like my Lady Fadler and Sir Francis: nor go to Hyde Park together the first Sunday in a new chariot, to provoke eyes and whispers; and then never be seen there together again; as if we were proud of one another the first week, and ashamed of one another ever after. Let us never visit together, nor go to a play together, but let us be very strange and wellbred: let us be as strange as if we had been married a great while; and as wellbred as if we were not married at all.

MIRA: Have you any more conditions to offer? Hitherto your demands are pretty reasonable.

MILLA: Trifles, – as liberty to pay and receive visits to and from whom I please; to write and receive letters, without interrogatories or wry faces on your part; to wear what I please; and choose conversation with regard only to my own taste; to have no obligation upon me to converse with wits that I don't like, because they are your acquaintance; or to be intimate with fools, because they may be your relations. Come to dinner when I please, dine in my dressing-room when I'm out of humour, without giving a reason. To have my closet inviolate; to be sole empress of my tea-table, which you must never presume to approach without first asking leave. And lastly wherever I am, you shall always knock at the door before you come in. These articles subscribed, if I continue to endure you a little longer, I may by degrees dwindle into a wife.

MIRA: Your bill of fair is something advanced in this latter account. Well, have I liberty to offer conditions – that when you are dwindled into a wife, I may not be beyond measure enlarged into a husband.

MILLA: You have free leave, propose your utmost, speak and spare not.

MIRA: I thank you. Imprimis then, I convenant that your acquaintance be general; that you admit no sworn confidante, or intimate of your own sex; no she friend to screen her affairs under your countenance, and tempt you to make trial of a mutual secrecy. No decoy-duck to wheedle you a fop – scrambling to the play in a mask – then bring you home in a pretended fright, when you think you shall be found out – and rail at me for missing the play, and disappointing the frolic which you had to pick me up and prove my constancy.

MILLA: Detestable Imprimis! I go to the play in a mask!

MIRA: Item, I article that you continue to like your own face, as long as I shall: and while it passes current with me, that you endeavour not to new coin it. To which end, together with all vizards for the day, I prohibit all masks for the night, made of oiled-skins and I know not what – hog's bones, hare's gall, pig water, and the marrow of a roasted cat. In short, I forbid all commerce with the gentlewomen in what-d'ye-call-it Court. Item, I shut my doors against all bawds with baskets, and penny-worth of muslin, china, fans, atlases, &c. – Item, when you shall be breeding –

MILLA: Ah! Name it not.

MIRA: Which may be presumed, with a blessing on our endeavours –

MILLA: Odious endeavours!

MIRA: I denounce against all strait lacing, squeezing for a shape, till you mould my boy's head like a sugar-loaf; and instead of a man-child, make me father to a crooked billet. Lastly, to the dominion of the tea-table I submit. – But with proviso, that you exceed not in your province; but restrain yourself to native and simple tea-table drinks, as tea, chocolate, and coffee. As likewise to genuine and authorized tea-table talk – such as mending of fashions, spoiling reputations, railing at absent friends, and so forth – but that on no account you encroach upon the men's prerogative, and presume to drink healths, or toast fellows; for prevention of which, I banish all foreign forces, all auxiliaries to the tea-table, as orange-brandy, all aniseed, cinnamon, citron and Barbadoes-water, together with ratafia and the most noble spirit of clary. – But for cowslip-wine, poppy-water, and all dormitives, those I allow. – These provisoes admitted, in other things I may prove a tractable and complying husband.

MILLA: O horrid provisoes! Filthy strong waters! I toast fellows, odious men! I hate your odious provisoes.

MIRA: Then we're agreed. Shall I kiss your hand upon the contract? And here comes one to be a witness to the sealing of the deed.

CHAPTER SIX

Some Ways to Promote Standardization

This chapter is an epilogue to our chronicle of famous mistakes and how to avoid them. That any epilogue should be necessary arises from what may have been overly great stress on individual coping with Contract English. People generally deal with contracts on an individual or a company basis, but collective onslaught against Babel is not out of the question either. Can anything be done on a grander scale? It seems unreasonable that everyone should have to learn a smattering of law and a new prose style to get through industrial negotiations. Somewhere there must be or ought to be learned academies giving fixed meanings to words and phrases that all of us use daily. So goes the argument; many of the problems explored earlier suggest it, and it affords the double enticement of leaving the hard questions to somebody else and appearing to make good common sense at the same time. Whether and in what degree it can be accomplished is next explored.

Non-English and Simpler English

The first thought that occurs is to avoid English altogether as too complex and conducive of cultural bias as the result of history. What about Esperanto?

A second notion is to work out contracts in Basic English, which has a limited vocabulary that was favored by Churchill and others concerned with enlarging the bonds uniting English-speaking peoples.

A third is to create something new with a computer.

All such "panglobalingual" fantasies are suspect without even fair consideration of the merits. Manchu and Basque, for all we know, may be as rich conceptually as English, but history says this is not the way things are going and that puts an end to it. English is here to stay for a time, not straitjacketed or restructured for sociological reasons but thriving as people use it by choice, rich and assimilative, turning up everywhere in its slovenly grandeur.

The social scientist is no match for the peasant going his own way while Icarus falls into the sea in Pieter Brueghel the Elder's masterpiece.

Industrial Glossaries

A more modest approach is to draft international rules for the interpretation of specific trade terms. The International Chamber of Commerce has done that, publishing material in English and French dealing with phrases such as "Ex Ship" and "Warehouse to Warehouse." The result was called "Incoterms," and the purpose was

> to provide a set of international rules for the interpretation of the chief terms used in foreign trade contracts, for the optional use of businessmen who prefer the certainty of uniform international rules to the uncertainties of the varied interpretations of the same terms in different countries.

The word "businessmen," incidentally ("hommes d'affaires" in the French text), reminds us of the need to invent new contract words suitable to either gender without the usual paragraph explaining that "his" can mean "hers" and so forth wherever the context admits it. "His or her" is no good either, nor even "her or his," because if you keep repeating that sort of thing you can get into a desperate muddle. Somebody will have to invent sexless pronouns such as "hs." for "his or hers," "e." for "he or she," and perhaps "rm." for "her or him." A more Latinate word like "Suo" with no declensions might combine all of these things, but it would scarcely be English.

A French-English glossary of legal terms in European treaties published in London, Berlin, and Munich by the Institut International de Terminologie juridique et administrative brings into its definitions entire bits of substantive law that relate to but transcend contracts, e.g., " secret professionnel":

> French law differs from the law of the United Kingdom in imposing an obligation of professional secrecy on a very large number of persons and if they do divulge secrets communicated to them or ascertained by them in the course of their professional duties, except where the law specifically provides to the contrary, they are liable to imprisonment . . . and a fine. . . .
>
> These persons include *inter alios:*
>
> members of the Judiciary
> a large number of specified officials
> doctors of medicine
> surgeons
> other medical practitioners (autres officiers de santé)
> chemists
> midwives
> notaries
> detective inspectors (inspecteurs de la sûreté)
> postal officials
> R.C. priests in respect of confessions
> police officers in respect of the names of informants.

It requires little imagination to accept how useful this sort of background can be in contract dealings that might involve different systems of law. Heavy industry is the main beneficiary, but even the private citizen may profit by knowing that French midwives must keep still without twenty contract clauses requiring them to do so.

Codes

If particular words and phrases can be standardized, why not entire concepts? There is logic in that notion, although it may collide with psychology.

Consider for example the difficulties that arise in drafting this important clause: "This agreement may not be altered, extended, or terminated, except for material breach or as elsewhere provided herein, without a writing to that effect signed on the same page by each of the parties hereto, and only in a document running one to the other with no third party as cosignatory." No normal person or even a German law scholar with several doctorates can toss that one off without torture. But what if he or she (or "e.") finds it all done for her or him (or "rm.") in a code book that is already his or hers (or "hs.")? That whole clause, with its Anglo-American legal underpinning, might be available in a prearranged single code word, such as "Tiberius," or merely four X's. The parties, of course, would have to agree in advance to the use of any such code and signal clearly when they were coming into and out of it.

Coded concepts offer intriguing possibilities, but in the long run they appear more likely to promote rather than diminish confusion. Even the trade glossaries must have limited scope. You simply cannot get everyone to agree forever on fixed meanings. Verbal petrification goes against human nature.

Summary

Trade glossaries can be useful in clarifying if not freezing certain expressions of interest to particular industries. Beyond that it will more likely than not be unsafe to go. The creation of elaborate contract code language to diminish misunderstanding and litigation may in the long run increase both.

In this field, as in so many others, the hard way is best. Thought that precedes speech and reasonable care in the choice of words—these are what will protect you in the transaction of serious affairs. Too much spontaneity is for songbirds, but the alternative is something better than computers. The alternative is self-discipline enriched by just a little study. It may even be that Contract English deserves a place in the school curriculum, and at an earlier stage than that which is considered appropriate for the study of law. The making and the honoring of agreements is part of universal experience. The subject is just as relevant as sex training and urban renewal. If it happens to be less fashionable, and not in the least trendy, those are impediments that do not always, according to history, prove overwhelming.

And so we conclude that choosing words for agreements is like marriage, both institutions being under a cloud but having this additional feature in common: that you are supposed to live with your choice. It follows that care in the selection ranks among the soundest of investments.

Here we conclude Part I of this book, in which various rules and examples have made up the text. Rules and examples, however, take you only so far in the study of any language, and so with Contract English as with Spanish or Indonesian it becomes essential to practice by reading entire specimens intact.

Accordingly Part II consists of sample agreements in English. A brief introductory note is followed by models which will repay study. In one case German and French versions are presented with the English text so that the reader may compare treatment of the same concepts in different languages. These are real contracts, not forms.

The documents in Part II are excellently structured, but nothing is perfect. They can best be read first with envy, then with the reader's critical faculties at work. What does this clause mean, and could the point have been put better? Is something important left unsaid, and is this likely to have resulted from disagreement or inadvertence? Asking yourself questions of this kind is good training.

Then, hearing new harmony in these things, you may be tempted to create your own, but the ultimate wisdom is knowing when to call in the professionals for guidance.

PART TWO

The following treaties were chosen as texts exemplifying commendable Contract English. Where French and German versions are presented alongside the English, readers able to deal with those languages may find it interesting to compare alternate wordings of the same concept.

These treaties are not to be placed under the microscope or brooded over in each detail, as we have done with the words and phrases presented earlier in this book. Rather, they are meant to be read straight through so that their architecture and music form a general impression. They reflect how literate people construct things with care.

And yet nobody striding through prose gardens can forget about pitfalls. Here are two last examples, not connected with the treaties in any way, to remind us how much good can be undone in the end game.

The first example might be entitled The Death or Mysterious Disappearance of the Subjunctive. In England, especially, the subjunctive is nearly extinct. If you seriously believe that only a few pedants and dons should mourn its passing, consider this case: an insurance company writes to one of its policyholders, "It is important that fire and theft are covered." The company means, of course, that they "be covered," not "are covered" in our hypothetical case where no such coverage has been laid on at all. The recipient of this letter assumes the opposite, thinking that "are covered" means what it says. Fire and theft ensue, then litigation when the truth comes out. Not every tragedy is like *Macbeth* and comes about as the result of murderous ambition. Lesser tragedies occur daily, and the cause is illiteracy.

The second example of a pitfall is subtler. It brings us a little closer to the following treaties in different languages, but only on the surface when you consider the position closely, because we have had something like this before and want only a reminder that translation from one language to another may be a disguise for deeper difficulties. Suppose the publishers of this book wanted the right to get out of the whole affair and withhold payment of the balance of an advance against royalties if they disliked the completed manuscript. They might stipulate payment of the remaining advance "on acceptance of the manuscript in final form and content satisfactory to the publisher." Finally—and here we approach the treaty area—with a French or Swiss author they might require a contract in French. How do you say "in final form and content satisfactory to the publisher" in French? A good way is "en bonne et due forme et avec texte definitif à l'entière satisfaction de l'editeur." Checking the translation, however, only touches the surface. The real problem, in English as well as French, is whether the legal systems underlying those languages permit the publishers arbitrarily to reject the manuscript for no good reason whatsoever.

In many instances they do not; an implication of reasonableness is read into the phrase, with the result that the author may have valid grounds for a lawsuit unless both the English and French are rephrased. Either the publishers must spell out that they can behave unreasonably, or restructure the whole contract in terms of options to go forward, or best of all undertake to behave reasonably and let the language stand as it is. The point, however, is that more than translation is involved. You can write the same clause in Afrikaans or Tamil, but you will be on unsafe ground unless you know something about the legal system behind it and whether its rules would govern the text of the particular contract in question.

Enough about quicksand. We move on to more congenial footing and take up Contract English at a higher level. The treaties that follow come in one sense as a reward for hard work in learning the equivalent of conjugations in language study.

Only now can we read Vergil.

BUNDESGESETZBLATT

FÜR DIE REPUBLIK ÖSTERREICH

Jahrgang 1971 | Ausgegeben am 31. März 1971 | 35. Stück

104. Europäische Übereinkunft über Formerfordernisse bei Patentanmeldungen samt Anlagen

104.

Der Bundespräsident erklärt die am 19. Jänner 1971 in Straßburg unterzeichnete Europäische Übereinkunft über Formerfordernisse bei Patentanmeldungen, welche also lautet:

EUROPEAN CONVENTION RELATING TO THE FORMALITIES REQUIRED FOR PATENT APPLICATIONS

The Governments signatory hereto, being Members of the Council of Europe,

Considering that the aim of the Council of Europe is to achieve greater unity between its Members for the purpose, among others, of facilitating their economic and social progress by agreements and common action in economic, social, cultural, scientific, legal and administrative matters;

Considering that it is in the general interest to simplify and unify as far as possible the formalities prescribed by the various national legislations in respect of applications for patents;

Having regard to Article 15 of the International Convention for the Protection of Industrial Property signed at Paris on 20th March, 1883, revised at Brussels on 14th December, 1900, at Washington on 2nd June, 1911, at The Hague on 6th November, 1925 and at London on 2nd June, 1934,

Have agreed as follows:

CONVENTION EUROPÉENNE RELATIVE AUX FORMALITÉS PRESCRITES POUR LES DEMANDES DE BREVETS

Les Gouvernements signataires, Membres du Conseil de l'Europe,

Considérant que le but du Conseil de l'Europe est de réaliser une union plus étroite entre ses Membres, a fin notamment de favoriser le progrès économique et social par la conclusion d'accords et par l'adoption d'une action commune dans les domaines économique, social, culturel, scientifique, juridique et administratif;

Considérant qu'il est de l'intérêt général de simplifier et d'unifier, dans toute la mesure du possible, les formalités prescrites par les diverses législations nationales pour les demandes de brevets;

Vu l'article 15 de la Convention Internationale pour la Protection de la Propriété Industrielle, signée à Paris le 20 mars 1883, révisée à Bruxelles le 14 décembre 1900, à Washington le 2 juin 1911, à La Haye le 6 novembre 1925 et à Londres le 2 juin 1934,

Sont convenus de ce qui suit:

(Übersetzung)

EUROPÄISCHE ÜBEREINKUNFT ÜBER FORMERFORDERNISSE BEI PATENTANMELDUNGEN

In der Erwägung, daß der Europarat die Herstellung einer engeren Verbindung zwischen seinen Mitgliedern zur Aufgabe hat, insbesondere um den wirtschaftlichen und sozialen Fortschritt durch den Abschluß von Abkommen und durch gemeinsames Vorgehen auf den Gebieten der Wirtschaft, des Sozialwesens, der Kultur, der Wissenschaft, des Rechts und der Verwaltung zu fördern;

in der Erwägung, daß es im allgemeinen Interesse liegt, im Ausmaße des Möglichen die gesetzlichen Formvorschriften der einzelnen Länder für Patentanmeldungen zu vereinfachen und zu vereinheitlichen;

im Hinblick auf Artikel 15 der am 20. März 1883 in Paris unterzeichneten und am 14. Dezember 1900 in Brüssel, am 2. Juni 1911 in Washington, am 6. November 1925 im Haag und am 2. Juni 1934 in London revidierten Verbandsübereinkunft zum Schutze des gewerblichen Eigentums

sind die unterzeichneten Mitgliedsregierungen des Europarats wie folgt übereingekommen:

ARTICLE 1

1. An application for a patent in any Contracting State

(a) may be required to accord with the provisions of Article 2 of this Convention;

(b) shall not be denied its date of filing on formal grounds if it complies with the requirements specified in Article 3 of this Convention;

(c) shall, if it otherwise complies with the law of that Contracting State, not be refused, so long as the requirements specified in Articles 4 to 6 of this Convention are satisfied.

2. The Contracting States shall make no other formal requirements that those set out in this Convention, but a Contracting State may dispense with any of the requirements contained herein.

ARTICLE 1

1. Dans chacun des Etats Contractants une demande de brevet:

(a) pourra être soumise aux prescriptions de l'article 2 de la présente Convention;

(b) ne pourra, pour des raisons de forme, perdre sa date de dépôt si elle satisfait aux exigences spécifiées à l'article 3 de la présente Convention;

(c) ne sera pas rejetée si elle satisfait aux exigences specifiées aux articles 4 à 6 de la présente Convention, les autres exigences légales étant respectées.

2. Les Etats contractants ne pourront imposer d'autres prescriptions de forme que celles découlant de la présente Convention. Ils pourront toutefois ne pas exiger l'observation de la totalité de ces prescriptions.

ARTIKEL 1

1. In jedem der Vertragsstaaten:

(a) kann eine Patentanmeldung den Bestimmungen des Artikels 2 dieser Übereinkunft unterworfen werden;

(b) kann eine solche Anmeldung, sofern sie den in Artikel 3 dieser Übereinkunft angegebenen Erfordernissen entspricht, nicht aus Formgründen ihr Anmeldungsdatum verlieren;

(c) darf eine solche Anmeldung, wenn sie den in Artikel 4 bis 6 dieser Übereinkunft angegebenen Erfordernissen entspricht, nicht zurückgewiesen werden, sofern die sonstigen Rechtsvorschriften beachtet sind.

2. Die Vertragsstaaten dürfen keine anderen Formvorschriften erlassen als diejenigen, welche sich aus dieser Übereinkunft ergeben. Sie können jedoch von einzelnen dieser Erfordernisse absehen.

ARTICLE 2

1. The applicant for a patent may be required to submit:

(a) an application form; a Contracting State may, however, require this form in duplicate;

(b) a specification of the invention in duplicate; a Contracting State which makes use of a system of examination for novelty may, however, require this specification in triplicate;

(c) drawings necessary for the understanding of the specification, in duplicate, or, if the law of the country in which the

ARTICLE 2

1. Le demandeur en brevet pourra être tenu de déposer:

(a) une requête; les Etats Contractants peuvent en exiger deux exemplaires;

(b) une description de l'invention en deux exemplaires; les États Contractants qui procèdent ou font procéder à l'examen de nouveauté des demandes de brevets peuvent en exiger trois exemplaires;

(c) les dessins nécessaires à l'intelligence de la description, en deux exemplaires, ou, si la loi du pays où la demande est

ARTIKEL 2

1. Es kann vorgeschrieben werden, daß der Patentsucher folgende Unterlagen einzureichen hat:

(a) einen Antrag; die Vertragsstaaten können diesen in zwei Stücken verlangen;

(b) eine Beschreibung der Erfindung in zwei Stücken; die Vertragsstaaten, die eine Prüfung der angemeldeten Patente auf ihre Neuheit vornehmen oder vornehmen lassen, können die Vorlage von drei Stücken verlangen;

(c) die zum Verständnis der Beschreibung notwendigen Zeichnungen in zwei oder, wenn es in dem Lande, in dem die Anmeldung er-

application is made requires it, in triplicate;

(d) such samples as the law of the country in which the application is made requires;

(e) if an agent is employed, a document proving his authorisation to act as such, and, if the law of the country in which application is made requires it, his acceptance of the authorisation; no legalisation or certification shall be necessary for this document;

(f) if the applicant is not himself the inventor according to the law of the country in which the application is made, and if such law requires it, a document proving his status, such as assignee of the inventor, or the assent of the inventor to the making of the application by an assignee;

(g) the fees required for an application or proof that they have been paid.

2. The application form and the accompanying documents shall be written in the language of, or in a language recognised for the purpose by, the country in which the application is made. The specification filed in support of an application for a patent or certificate of addition may be required to be in the same language as the application for the main patent.

ARTICLE 3

1. An application shall not be denied its date filing on formal grounds if the application form, though it does not comply with the requirements of Article 4, is filed accompanied by:

déposée l'exige, en trois exemplaires;

(d) les échantillons requis par la loi du pays où la demande est déposée;

(e) s'il est constitué un mandataire, un pouvoir, accepté formellement par celui-ci, si la loi du pays où la demande est déposée l'exige; aucune légalisation ni certification du pouvoir n'est nécessaire;

(f) si le déposant n'est pas lui-même l'inventeur au sens de la loi du pays où la demande est déposée, et si cette loi l'exige, un document prouvant la qualité en laquelle il agit, telle que celle d'ayant droit de l'inventeur, ou l'assentiment de l'inventeur au dépôt de la demande par un ayant droit;

(g) le montant des taxes exigées pour le dépôt ou la preuve de leur paiement.

2. La requête et ses annexes seront rédigées dans la langue du pays ou dans une des langues admises à cet effet par le pays où la demande est déposée. Il pourra être exigé que la description déposée à l'appui d'une demande de brevet ou de certificat d'addition soit rédigée dans la même langue que celle de la demande du brevet principal.

ARTICLE 3

1. Le bénéfice de la date de dépôt ne sera pas refusé pour des raisons de forme, si la requête, même non conforme aux prescriptions de l'article 4, est accompagnée:

folgt, gesetzlich vorgeschrieben ist, in drei Stücken;

(d) die in dem Land, in dem die Anmeldung erfolgt, gesetzlich vorgeschriebenen Muster;

(e) im Falle der Bestellung eines Bevollmächtigten eine Vollmacht, die von ihm ausdrücklich anzunehmen ist, falls dies in einem Lande, in dem die Anmeldung erfolgt, gesetzlich vorgeschrieben ist; eine Beglaubigung oder Bestätigung der Vollmacht ist nicht erforderlich;

(f) wenn der Anmelder nach dem Recht des Landes, in dem die Anmeldung erfolgt, nicht selbst der Erfinder ist und wenn dieses Recht es vorschreibt, einen schriftlichen Nachweis der Eigenschaft, in welcher er handelt, z. B. als Rechtsnachfolger des Erfinders, oder die Einwilligung des Erfinders zur Anmeldung durch einen Rechtsnachfolger;

(g) den Betrag der für die Anmeldung vorgeschriebenen Gebühren oder den Nachweis ihrer Entrichtung.

2. Der Antrag und die dazugehörigen Anlagen sind in der Sprache des Landes, in dem die Anmeldung erfolgt, oder in einer von diesem hierfür zugelassenen Sprache abzufassen. Es kann vorgeschrieben werden, daß die als Unterlage für die Anmeldung eines Zusatzpatents oder für den Antrag auf eine Zusatzbescheinigung eingereichte Beschreibung in derselben Sprache wie die Anmeldung des Hauptpatents zu erfolgen hat.

ARTIKEL 3

1. Die Zuerkennung des Anmeldedatums darf nicht aus Formgründen versagt werden, wenn dem Antrag — selbst wenn er nicht den Bestimmungen des Artikels 4 entspricht — beiliegen:

(a) one copy of a specification of the invention in the language of, or in a language recognised for the purpose by, the country in which the application is made, even though that specification does not comply with the requirements of Article 5;

(b) one copy of the drawings where necessary for the understanding of the specification, even though those drawings do not comply with the requirements of Article 6;

(c) the amount of the fees or proof that they have been paid.

2. The law of the country in which application is made may fix time-limits within which the other documents mentioned in Article 2 shall be filed or the documents already filed shall be regularised.

3. The Contracting States shall permit applications to be sent by post, provided that nothing in this paragraph shall affect the validity of any laws of any Contracting State relating to the requirement of an agent or of an address for service.

ARTICLE 4

1. The application form shall be regarded as formally in order, as regards its size and the kind of paper used, if is made on strong white paper of a size of 29 to 34 cms. by 20 to 22 cms.

2. The application form shall be regarded as formally in order as regards its contents if it is properly made on one of the standard application forms annexed to this Convention, or if it complies with the provisions of paragraph 2 of Article 2 and contains:

(a) the surname and first names (or in the case of a

(a) d'un exemplaire de la description dans la langue du pays ou dans une langue admise à cet effet par le pays où la demande est déposée, même si cette description n'est pas conforme aux prescriptions de l'article 5;

(b) d'un exemplaire des dessins nécessaires à l'intelligence de la description, même si ces dessins ne sont pas conformes aux prescriptions de l'article 6;

(c) du montant des taxes ou de la preuve de leur paiement.

2. La législation du pays où la demande est faite peut fixer les délais dans lesquels devront être déposés les autres documents mentionnés dans l'article 2, ou devront être régularisés les documents déjà déposés.

3. Les Etats Contractants autoriseront l'envoi postal des demandes, sans préjudice de toute réglementation nationale concernant l'exigence d'un mandataire ou d'une élection de domicile.

ARTICLE 4

1. La requête sera considérée comme régulière en la forme, quant au format et à la nature du papier utilisé, si elle est établie sur papier fort et blanc, du format de 29 à 34 cm sur 20 à 22 cm.

2. La requête sera considérée comme régulière en la forme, en ce qui concerne ses énonciations, si elle est faite sur l'une des formules-types de requête annexées à la présente Convention ou si elle répond aux prescriptions de l'article 2, paragraphe 2, et contient:

(a) l'indication des nom et prénoms (la raison sociale

(a) ein Stück der Beschreibung der Erfindung in der Sprache des Landes, in dem die Anmeldung erfolgt, oder in einer von diesem hierfür zugelassenen Sprache auch dann, wenn diese Beschreibung nicht den Bestimmungen des Artikels 5 entspricht;

(b) ein Stück der zum Verständnis der Beschreibung erforderlichen Zeichnungen auch dann, wenn diese Zeichnungen nicht den Bestimmungen des Artikels 6 entsprechen;

(c) der Betrag der Gebühren oder der Nachweis ihrer Entrichtung.

2. Das Recht des Landes, in dem die Anmeldung erfolgt, kann die Fristen bestimmen, innerhalb deren die in Artikel 2 erwähnten anderen Unterlagen einzureichen bzw. die bereits eingereichten Unterlagen in die vorgeschriebene Form zu bringen sind.

3. Die Vertragsstaaten lassen die Übermittlung der Anmeldungen durch die Post zu, unbeschadet etwaiger nationaler Rechtsvorschriften über das Erfordernis eines Bevollmächtigten oder der Begründung eines Zustellungswohnsitzes.

ARTIKEL 4

1. Der Antrag gilt hinsichtlich des Formats und der Art des verwendeten Papiers als formgerecht, wenn er auf kräftigem weißen Papier in der Größe von 29 bis 34 cm mal 20 bis 22 cm gestellt ist.

2. Der Antrag gilt hinsichtlich seines Inhalts als formgerecht, wenn er auf einem Antragsformular gestellt wird, das dem dieser Übereinkunft beigefügten Muster oder den Bestimmungen von Artikel 2 Absatz 2 entspricht und enthält:

(a) Namen und Vornamen (bei einer Gesellschaft

body corporate, the name), nationality, domicile or registered office and complete address of the applicant;

(b) the full name and address of the agent, if there is one;

(c) a short and precise title for the invention, without any fancy names;

(d) if the law of the country in which application is made requires it, a declaration stating that the applicant is the true and first inventor or the assignee thereof;

(e) a statement whether the applicant requires an independent patent, a patent of importation, a patent for an improvement or a patent or certificate of addition or whether his application is a divisional application. There shall also be given the number of the patent, or of the application for the patent, to which the application for a patent for an improvement, or for a patent or certificate of addition or the divisional application relates;

(f) if there are several applicants and no common agent, the name of the person to whom official communications are to be addressed;

(g) the signature of the applicant or that of his agent, if, under the law of the country in which the application is made, the latter is empowered by the applicant to sign. If two application forms are

ou de commerce, s'il s'agit d'une société), nationalité, domicile ou siège social et adresse complète du déposant;

(b) l'indication complète des nom et adresse du mandataire, s'il en a été constitué un;

(c) la désignation précise et sommaire de l'invention, sans aucune dénomination de fantaisie;

(d) si la loi du pays où la demande est déposée l'exige, une déclaration portant que le déposant est le véritable et premier inventeur, ou l'ayant droit du véritable et premier inventeur;

(e) la déclaration soit que la demande tend à l'obtention d'un brevet principal, d'un brevet d'importation, d'un brevet de perfectionnement, d'un brevet additionel ou d'un certificat d'addition, soit qu'il s'agit d'une demande divisionnaire. On indiquera le numéro du brevet ou de la demande du brevet auquel la demande du brevet de perfectionnement, du brevet additionnel, du certificat d'addition ou la demande divisionnaire se réfère;

(f) s'il y a plusieurs déposants et s'il n'y a pas de mandataire commun, la désignation de la personne à laquelle doivent être envoyées les communications officielles;

(g) la signature du demandeur ou celle du mandataire, si ce dernier est habilité par le demandeur à signer la requête, conformément à la loi du pays où celle-ci est déposée. Si deux exemplaires de la requête

oder Handelsbezeichnung), Staatsangehörigkeit, Wohnsitz oder Gesellschaftssitz und vollständige Anschrift des Anmelders;

(b) vollen Namen und vollständige Anschrift des Bevollmächtigten, falls ein solcher bestellt ist;

(c) kurze und genaue Bezeichnung der Erfindung ohne jede Phantasiebenennung;

(d) wenn das Recht des Landes, in dem die Anmeldung erfolgt, es vorschreibt, eine Erklärung dahingehend, daß der Anmelder der wirkliche und erste Erfinder oder dessen Rechtsnachfolger ist;

(e) eine Erklärung, aus der hervorgeht, daß mit der Anmeldung die Erteilung eines Hauptpatents, eines Einführungspatents, eines Verbesserungspatents, eines Zusatzpatents oder einer Zusatzbescheinigung begehrt wird oder daß es sich um eine ausgeschiedene Anmeldung handelt. Die Nummer des Patents oder der Patentanmeldung, auf welche sich die Anmeldung des Verbesserungspatents, des Zusatzpatents oder der Antrag auf Erteilung einer Zusatzbescheinigung oder die ausgeschiedene Anmeldung bezieht, ist anzugeben;

(f) bei Vorhandensein mehrerer Anmelder und Fehlen eines gemeinsamen Bevollmächtigten, die Angabe der Person, an welche amtliche Mitteilungen zu richten sind;

(g) die Unterschrift des Anmelders oder des Bevollmächtigten, wenn dieser nach den Rechtsvorschriften des Landes, in dem die Anmeldung erfolgt, vom Anmelder zur Unterzeichnung des Antrags ermäch-

required, only one need be signed;

(h) if the law of the country in which application is made requires it, a list of the documents accompanying the application as set out in Article 2;

(i) an address for service in the country in which the application is made, if the applicant's address is outside the country and its law does not require that there be an agent therein.

ARTICLE 5

The specification shall be regarded as formally in order if it complies with the provisions of paragraph 2 of Article 2 and with the following conditions:

(a) it is written on one side only of one or more sheets of strong white paper, 29 to 34 cms. long and 20 to 22 cms. wide; the sheets are connected together in such a way that they can be separated and re-united without causing any difficulty to the reader; and the pages are numbered;

(b) it is handwritten, typed, lithographed or printed, and easily legible, the ink being dark and indelible;

(c) a margin of about 3 or 4 cms. is left on the left-hand side of each sheet as well as spaces of about 8 cms. at the head of the first page and foot of the last;

sont exigés, un seul exemplaire devra être signé;

(h) si la loi du pays où la demande est déposée l'exige, la liste des pièces annexées à la requête et prévues à l'article 2;

(i) une adresse de service dans le pays où la demande est faite, si le demandeur n'y est pas domicilié, et si la loi de ce pays n'exige pas qu'un mandataire y soit constitué.

ARTICLE 5

La description sera considérée comme régulière en la forme dès lors qu'elle répondra aux prescriptions de l'article 2, paragraphe 2, et aux conditions ci-après:

(a) elle sera faite au recto d'une ou de plusieurs feuilles de papier fort et blanc, du format de 29 à 34 cm de hauteur sur 20 à 22 cm de largeur; les feuilles seront réunies en fascicule de façon qu'il soit possible de les séparer et de les réunir à nouveau sans qu'il résulte de leur mode de réunion aucune difficulté pour la lecture; les pages seront numérotées;

(b) elle sera faite à la main ou à la machine, ou lithographiée ou imprimée, de façon bien lisible, à l'encre foncée et inaltérable;

(c) une marge d'environ 3 ou 4 cm sera toujours réservée sur le côté gauche de la feuille, ainsi qu'un espace d'environ 8 cm au haut de la première page et au bas de la dernière;

tigt ist. Wird der Antrag in zwei Stücken verlangt, so genügt die Unterzeichnung eines Stükkes;

(h) wenn das Recht des Landes, in dem die Anmeldung erfolgt, es vorschreibt, eine Aufstellung der gemäß Artikel 2 beigefügten Anlagen;

(i) eine Zustellungsanschrift in dem Lande, in dem die Anmeldung erfolgt, wenn der Anmelder dort keinen Wohnsitz hat und die Bestellung eines Bevollmächtigten in diesem Lande nach Landesrecht nicht vorgeschrieben ist.

ARTIKEL 5

Die Beschreibung ist als formgerecht anzusehen, wenn sie den Bestimmungen des Artikels 2 Absatz 2 und den nachstehenden Bedingungen entspricht:

(a) sie soll einseitig auf einem oder mehreren Blättern kräftigen weißen Papiers im Format von 29 bis 34 cm Höhe und 20 bis 22 cm Breite geschrieben sein; die Blätter sind so miteinander zu verbinden, daß sie ohne Schwierigkeit für den Leser getrennt und wieder vereinigt werden können; die Seiten sind zu numerieren;

(b) sie ist mittels dunkler und haltbarer Tinte oder Farbe in Hand- oder Maschinenschrift, Lithographie oder Druck auszuführen und soll leicht lesbar sein;

(c) auf jedem Blatt ist links ein etwa 3 bis 4 cm breiter Rand und auf der ersten Seite oben sowie auf der letzten Seite unten ein Raum von etwa 8 cm freizulassen;

(d) a space sufficient to permit the interlineation of corrections is left between the lines;

(e) the specification does not contain drawings other than graphic chemical and mathematical formulae;

(f) units ot weights and measures are in accordance with the metric system, temperatures in degrees centigrade, and density as specific gravity; for electrical units the rules agreed by international practice are observed and for chemical formulae the symbols, atomic weights and molecular formulae in general use in the country in which the application is made are employed;

(g) the specification is reasonably free from erasures, alterations or over-writings, and any which do occur in the originally filed document are mentioned in the margin or recited at the end of the description and initialled, and are made in the same manner on all the copies;

(h) the heading recites the surname and first names of the applicant (or in the case of a body corporate, its name) and the title of the invention;

(i) one or more copies of the specification is or are signed by the applicant or his agent, according to the law of the country in which the application is made.

(d) entre les lignes, il sera laissé un espace suffisant pour permettre d'apposer des rectifications interlinéaires;

(e) la description ne contiendra pas de dessins, exception faite des formules graphiques développées chimiques ou mathématiques;

(f) les indications de poids et mesures seront données d'après le système métrique, les indications de température en degrés centigrades, la densité comme poids spécifique; pour les unités électriques, on observera les prescriptions admises dans la pratique internationale, et on utilisera, pour les formules chimiques, les symboles des éléments, les poids atomiques et les formules moléculaires généralement en usage dans le pays où la demande est déposée;

(g) la description sera, autant que possible, exempte de ratures, d'altérations ou de surcharges; celles qui apparaîtraient dans la rédaction originale seront mentionnées en marge ou citées à la fin de la description et paraphées; elles seront effectuées d'une manière identique sur tous les exemplaires;

(h) l'entête indiquera les nom et prénoms du demandeur (la raison sociale ou de commerce, s'il s'agit d'une société), ainsi que la designation de l'invention;

(i) un ou plusieurs exemplaires sera ou seront signés par le déposant ou par son mandataire, conformément aux dispositions de la loi du pays où la demande est déposée.

(d) zwischen den Zeilen ist genügend Raum für die Einfügung von Berichtigungen zu lassen;

(e) die Beschreibung soll, abgesehen von graphisch dargestellten, chemischen und mathematischen Formeln, keine Zeichnungen enthalten;

(f) Gewichts- und Maßangaben haben nach dem metrischen System, Temperaturangaben in Grad Celsius, Dichtenangaben als spezifisches Gewicht zu erfolgen; für elektrische Maßeinheiten sind die in der internationalen Praxis zugelassenen Vorschriften zu beachten und bei chemischen Formeln die Zeichen der Elemente, die Atomgewichte und die Molekularformeln, die in dem Lande, in dem die Anmeldung erfolgt, allgemein verwendet werden, zu benutzen;

(g) die Beschreibung hat möglichst frei von Radierungen, Änderungen und Überschreibungen zu sein; soweit sie im Original vorhanden sein sollten, sind sie am Rande zu vermerken oder am Ende der Beschreibung aufzuführen und abzuzeichnen; sie sind auf sämtlichen Stükken in gleicher Weise vorzunehmen;

(h) im Kopf des Schriftstückes sind Namen und Vornamen des Anmelders (bei einer Gesellschaft Firma oder Handelsbezeichnung) sowie die Bezeichnung der Erfindung aufzuführen;

(i) die Beschreibung ist auf einem oder mehreren Stücken gemäß den Rechtsvorschriften des Landes, in dem die Anmeldung erfolgt, vom Anmelder oder seinem Bevollmächtigten zu unterzeichnen.

ARTICLE 6

The drawings shall be regarded as formally in order if they comply with the following conditions:

(a) one of the copies of the drawings is made on one or more sheets of strong, non-shiny, flexible, transparent material. Not more than two other copies, exact replicas of the first, are supplied on strong, white, smooth, non-shiny paper; these copies may be good quality lithographs. If the copy on flexible, transparent material is made by means of a printing press, the other copies may be printed from the same block. Any Contracting State may, however, require that one of these latter copies shall bear no reference signs;

(b) each sheet is 29 to 34 cms. long by 21 cms. wide, or, exceptionally, 42 cms. wide. With sheets 21 cms. wide, the surface used is no more than 25.7 cms. by 17 cms.

(c) all parts of the drawings are executed in durable, dark (if possible, black) markings without colours or colour washes and lend themselves to simple photographic reproduction or to reproduction without any intermediary steps on a stereotype;

(d) sections are indicated by oblique hatching which does not impede the clear reading of the reference signs and leading lines;

ARTICLE 6

Les dessins seront considérés comme réguliers en la forme dès lors qu'ils répondront aux conditions ci-après:

(a) un des exemplaires des dessins sera exécuté sur une ou plusieurs feuilles de matière transparente, souple, résistante et non brillante. Deux autres exemplaires au plus, reproduisant exactement le premier, seront exécutés sur papier blanc, fort, lisse et non brillant; ces derniers exemplaires pourront consister en copies lithographiques de bonne qualité. Se l'exemplaire sur feuille de matière transparente et souple est reproduit à l'aide d'un procédé d'impression, les autres exemplaires pourront être imprimés au moyen du même cliché. Les Etats Contractants pourront toutefois exiger que l'un de ces derniers exemplaires ne porte aucun signe de référence;

(b) le format de chaque feuille sera de 29 à 34 cm de hauteur sur 21 cm, et exceptionnellement 42 cm de largeur, la surface utile, dans le cas où il est fait usage du format de 21 cm de largeur, n'étant pas supérieure à 25,7 cm sur 17 cm;

(c) le dessin sera exécuté dans toutes ses parties en traits foncés (si possible noirs), durables, sans lavis ni couleurs, et devra se prêter à la reproduction nette par la photographie ou à la reproduction sans intermédiaire sur un stéréotype;

(d) les coupes seront indiquées par des hachures obliques; celles-ci ne devront pas empêcher de reconnaître clairement les signes et traits de référence;

ARTIKEL 6

Die Zeichnungen sind als formgerecht anzusehen, wenn sie den nachstehenden Erfordernissen entsprechen:

(a) ein Stück der Zeichnung ist auf einem oder mehreren Blättern aus durchsichtigem, biegsamem, widerstandsfähigem und mattem Material auszuführen. Höchstens zwei weitere, dem ersten genau entsprechende Stücke sind auf kräftigem, glattem und mattem weißen Papier auszuführen; diese letztgenannten Stücke können aus guten lithographischen Abzügen bestehen. Ist das Stück auf durchsichtigem und biegsamem Material im Wege eines Druckverfahrens hergestellt, so können die anderen Stücke mit demselben Klischee gedruckt werden. Die Vertragsstaaten können jedoch verlangen, daß eines dieser letztgenannten Stücke keinerlei Hinweiszeichen enthält;

(b) jedes Blatt soll ein Format von 29 bis 34 cm Höhe und 21 cm — ausnahmsweise 42 cm — Breite haben. Bei Benutzung des Formats von 21 cm Breite soll die benutzte Fläche 25,7 cm mal 17 cm nicht überschreiten;

(c) die Zeichnung ist in allen Teilen mit dunklen (möglichst schwarzen) dauerhaften Strichen ohne Farben oder Farbtuschung auszuführen und soll sich zur klaren photographischen Wiedergabe oder zur Wiedergabe ohne Zwischenstufen auf Stereotypplatte eignen;

(d) Schnitte sind durch Schrägschraffierung zu kennzeichnen; diese darf die klare Erkennbarkeit der Hinweiszeichen und -linien nicht beeinträchtigen;

(e) the scale of the drawings in such that, depending on the degree of complexity of the figure, a photographic reproduction with a linear reduction in size to two-thirds allows all the detail to be seen without difficulty; and, if the scale is shown on the drawings, it is drawn and not indicated in writing;

(f) the different figures are clearly separated one from another, arranged on as few sheets as possible and numbered continuously and independently of the number of sheets;

(g) all numbers, letters and reference lines appearing on the drawings are simple and clear, the letters and numbers being at least 0.32 cms. high; and each item depicted in the figures, insofar as the understanding of the specification requires it, is denoted by the same reference letter or number throughout and these agree with those used in the specification;

(h) the drawings do not contain explanatory matter with the exception of such terms as "water", "steam", "section on AB", "open", "shut", and, in the case of electric block schematic diagrams and flow sheet diagrams, explanatory matter sufficient to enable them to be understood, when such terms and explanatory matter appear in the language of, or in a language recognised for the purpose by, the country in which the application is filed;

(e) l'échelle des dessins sera déterminée par le degré de complication des figures; elle sera telle qu'une reproduction photographique effectuée avec une réduction linéaire aux deux tiers permette de distinguer sans peine tous les détails; lorsqu'elle sera portée sur le dessin, elle sera dessinée et non indiquée par une mention écrite;

(f) les diverses figures seront nettement séparées les unes des autres, disposées sur un nombre de feuilles aussi réduit que possible et numérotées d'une manière continue et sans tenir compte du nombre des feuilles;

(g) tous les chiffres, lettres et signes de référence figurant dans les dessins seront simples et nets; les lettres et chiffres auront une hauteur de 0,32 cm au moins. Les différentes parties des figures, dans la mesure où l'exigera l'intelligence de la description, seront désignées partout par les mêmes signes de référence, concordant avec ceux de la description;

(h) le dessin ne contiendra aucune explication, à l'exception de légendes telles que « eau », « vapeur », « coupe suivant AB », « ouvert », « fermé » et, pour les schémas d'installations électriques ou les diagrammes schématisant les étapes d'un processus de traitement, les mentions suffisantes pour les expliquer; ces légendes et mentions devront être rédigées dans la langue du pays ou l'une des langues admises à cet effet par le pays où la demande est déposée;

(e) der Maßstab der Zeichnungen richtet sich nach dem Grade der Kompliziertheit der Abbildungen; er ist so zu halten, daß eine photographische Wiedergabe unter linearer Verkleinerung auf zwei Drittel das mühelose Erkennen aller Einzelheiten gestattet; wird der Maßstab auf der Zeichnung erwähnt, so hat dies zeichnerisch und nicht schriftlich zu geschehen;

(f) die einzelnen Abbildungen sind klar voneinander zu trennen, auf einer möglichst geringen Anzahl von Blättern unterzubringen und fortlaufend ohne Rücksicht auf die Seitenzahl zu numerieren;

(g) alle Ziffern, Buchstaben und Hinweiszeichen in den Zeichnungen sollen einfach und klar sein; die Buchstaben und Ziffern sollen mindestens 0,32 cm hoch sein. Die verschiedenen Teile der Abbildungen sind, soweit es für das Verständnis der Beschreibung erforderlich ist, überall mit denselben Hinweiszeichen, die mit denen der Beschreibung übereinstimmen, zu bezeichnen;

(h) die Zeichnungen sollen keine Erläuterungen enthalten, ausgenommen Angaben wie „Wasser", „Dampf", „Schnitt nach AB", „offen", „zu", und bei elektrischen Blockschaltbildern und Diagrammen, die den Ablauf eines Verfahrens schematisch wiedergeben, zu ihrem Verständnis ausreichende Angaben; diese Arten von Angaben sind in der Sprache des Landes, in dem die Anmeldung erfolgt, oder in einer von diesem hierfür zugelassenen Sprache abzufassen;

(i) each sheet carries in the margin the name of the applicant, the total number of sheets with the number of each sheet, and the signature of the applicant or his agent;

(j) the drawings are filed in such a way as to be from creases or cracks unfavourable to photographic reproduction.

ARTICLE 7

1. In each Contracting State any person desiring to take advantage, under the Convention of Paris for the Protection of Industrial Property, of the priority of a previous application shall enjoy a period of at least two months, starting from the subsequent application, to make a declaration to this effect. Each Contracting State, however, reserves the right to prescribe that this declaration should be made within the priority period laid down by that Convention.

2. When a declaration of priority is made in accordance with paragraph 1 of this Article, the applicant may be required to submit a certified copy of the specification and drawings of the original application and such other documents as the law of the country in which the subsequent application is made may require.

3. Insofar as the documents referred to in paragraph 2 of this Article are drawn up in English, French or German or accompanied by an officially certified translation in one of these languages, it shall not be necessary to provide a translation in the language of, or in a language recognised for the purpose by, the country in which application is made, unless the competent authority requires it.

(i) chaque feuille portera en marge l'indication du nom du déposant et le nombre total des feuilles avec le numéro de la feuille même, ainsi que la signature du déposant ou celle du mandataire;

(j) les dessins seront déposés de manière à ne présenter ni pli ni cassure défavorables à la reproduction photographique.

ARTICLE 7

1. Dans chacun des États Contractants, quiconque voudra se prévaloir, dans les termes de la Convention de Paris pour la Protection de la Propriété Industrielle, de la priorité d'un dépôt antérieur, jouira d'un délai de deux mois au moins à compter du dépôt ultérieur, pour en faire la déclaration. Chacun des Etats Contractants se réserve toutefois la faculté de prescrire que cette déclaration soit faite dans le délai de priorité prévu à ladite Convention.

2. Lorsqu'une déclaration de priorité sera faite dans les conditions prévues au paragraphe 1 du présent article, le demandeur pourra être requis de fournir une copie certifiée de la description et des dessins de la demande d'origine, et tout autre document qui pourrait être exigé par la loi du pays du dépôt ultérieur.

3. En ce qui concerne les documents mentionnés au paragraphe 2 du présent article et rédigés en allemand, anglais ou français, ou accompagnés d'une traduction officiellement certifiée conforme dans l'une de ces langues, il ne sera pas nécessaire de produire une traduction dans la langue du pays ou dans une langue admise à cet effet par le pays où est déposée la demande de brevet, à moins que l'autorité compétente ne l'exige.

(i) jedes Blatt hat am Rande den Namen des Anmelders und die Gesamtzahl der Blätter samt der Nummer des betreffenden Blattes sowie die Unterschrift des Anmelders oder des Bevollmächtigten zu tragen;

(j) die Zeichnungen sind ohne Falten oder Brüche, die der photographischen Wiedergabe abträglich sind, einzureichen.

ARTIKEL 7

1. Wer in einem Vertragsstaat auf Grund der Pariser Verbandsübereinkunft zum Schutze des gewerblichen Eigentums die Priorität einer vorhergehenden Anmeldung in Anspruch nehmen will, hat dies innerhalb einer Frist von mindestens zwei Monaten, vom Zeitpunkt der späteren Anmeldung an gerechnet, zu erklären. Jeder Vertragsstaat behält sich jedoch die Befugnis vor, zu bestimmen, daß diese Erklärung innerhalb der in der genannten Übereinkunft vorgesehenen Prioritätsfrist zu erfolgen hat.

2. Erfolgt eine Prioritätserklärung nach Maßgabe des Absatzes 1 dieses Artikels, so kann dem Anmelder auferlegt werden, eine beglaubigte Abschrift der Beschreibung und der Zeichnungen der ursprünglichen Anmeldung und jede weitere Unterlage beizubringen, die nach dem Recht des Landes der späteren Anmeldung gegebenenfalls vorgeschrieben ist.

3. Sind die in Absatz 2 dieses Artikels erwähnten Unterlagen in deutscher, englischer oder französischer Sprache abgefaßt oder ist ihnen eine amtlich beglaubigte Übersetzung in einer dieser Sprachen beigefügt, so braucht keine Übersetzung in die Sprache des Landes, in dem die Anmeldung erfolgt, oder in eine von diesem hierfür zugelassene Sprache vorgelegt zu werden, sofern die zuständige Behörde dies nicht verlangt.

ARTICLE 8

1. This Convention shall be open to the signature of the Members of the Council of Europe. It shall be ratified. Instruments of ratification shall be deposited with the Secretary-General of the Council of Europe.

2. This Convention shall come into force on the first day of the month following the date of deposit of the fourth instrument of ratification.

3. As regards any Signatory ratifying subsequently, the Convention shall come into force on the first day of the month following the date of the deposit of its instrument of ratification.

ARTICLE 9

1. After it has come into force, this Convention shall be open to accession by all States which are Members of the International Union for the Protection of Industrial Property.

2. Accession shall be effected by the deposit of an instrument of accession with the Secretary-General of the Council of Europe, which shall take effect on the first day of the month following the date of deposit.

ARTICLE 10

The Secretary-General of the Council of Europe shall notify to the Members of the Council, to any States which may have acceded to this Convention and to the Director of the International Bureau for the Protection of Industrial Property at Berne:

(a) the date of entry into force of this Convention and the names of any Members of the Council which ratify it;

(b) the deposit of any instruments of accession in accordance with Article 9;

ARTICLE 8

1. La présente Convention est ouverte à la signature des Membres du Conseil de l'Europe. Elle sera ratifiée. Les instruments de ratification seront déposés près le Secrétaire Général du Conseil de l'Europe.

2. La présente Convention entrera en vigueur le premier jour du mois suivant le dépôt du quatrième instrument de ratification.

3. Pour tout signataire qui la ratifiera ultérieurement, la Convention entrera en vigueur le premier jour du mois suivant le dépôt de son instrument de ratification.

ARTICLE 9

1. Après son entrée en vigueur, la présente Convention sera ouverte à l'adhésion de tout État membre de l'Union internationale pour la Protection de la Propriété Industrielle.

2. L'adhésion s'effectuera par le dépôt, près le Secrétaire Général du Conseil de l'Europe, d'un instrument d'adhésion qui prendra effet le premier jour du mois suivant son dépôt.

ARTICLE 10

Le Secrétaire Général du Conseil de l'Europe notifiera aux Membres du Conseil, aux États qui auront adhéré à la présente Convention ainsi qu'au Directeur du Bureau International de Berne pour la Protection de la Propriété Industrielle.

(a) la date de l'entrée en vigueur de la présente Convention et les noms des Membres du Conseil qui l'auront ratifiée;

(b) le dépôt de tout instrument d'adhésion effectué en application des dispositions de l'article 9;

ARTIKEL 8

1. Diese Übereinkunft steht den Mitgliedstaaten des Europarats zur Unterzeichnung offen. Sie bedarf der Ratifikation. Die Ratifikationsurkunden sind beim Generalsekretär des Europarats zu hinterlegen.

2. Diese Übereinkunft tritt mit dem ersten Tage des auf die Hinterlegung der vierten Ratifikationsurkunde folgenden Monats in Kraft.

3. Für jeden Unterzeichner, der sie später ratifiziert, tritt die Übereinkunft mit dem ersten Tage des auf die Hinterlegung seiner Ratifikationsurkunde folgenden Monats in Kraft.

ARTIKEL 9

1. Nach ihrem Inkrafttreten steht die Übereinkunft jedem Mitgliedstaat des Internationalen Verbandes zum Schutze des gewerblichen Eigentums zum Beitritt offen.

2. Der Beitritt erfolgt durch Hinterlegung einer Beitrittserklärung beim Generalsekretär des Europarats, die mit dem ersten Tage des darauffolgenden Monats wirksam wird.

ARTIKEL 10

Der Generalsekretär des Europarats teilt den Mitgliedern des Rats, den Staaten, die dieser Übereinkunft beigetreten sind, sowie dem Direktor des Internationalen Büros zum Schutze des gewerblichen Eigentums in Bern mit:

(a) den Tag des Inkrafttretens dieser Übereinkunft und die Namen der Mitglieder des Rats, die sie ratifiziert haben;

(b) die Hinterlegung jeder Beitrittserklärung gemäß Artikel 9;

(c) any notification received in accordance with Article 11.

ARTICLE 11

1. This Convention shall remain in force for an unlimited time.

2. Any Contracting State may denounce this Convention by giving one year's notice to this effect to the Secretary-General of the Council of Europe.

In witness whereof the undersigned, being duly authorised thereto, have signed this Convention.

Done at Paris, this 11th day of December, 1953, in the English and French languages, both texts being equally authoritative, in a single copy, which shall remain in the archives of the Council of Europe and of which the Secretary-General shall send certified copies to each of the signatory and acceding Governments and to the Director of the International Bureau for the Protection of Industrial Property at Berne.

(c) toute notification reçue en application des dispositions de l'article 11.

ARTICLE 11

1. La présente Convention demeurera en vigueur sans limitation de durée.

2. Tout État contractant pourra mettre fin, en ce qui le concerne, à l'application de la présente Convention en donnant un préavis d'un an à cet effet au Secrétaire Général du Conseil de l'Europe.

En foi de quoi, les soussignés, ont dûment autorisés à cet effet, signé la présente Convention.

Fait à Paris, le 11 décembre 1953, en français et en anglais, les deux textes faisant également foi, en un seul exemplaire, qui sera déposé dans les archives du Conseil de l'Europe. Le Secrétaire Général en communiquera des copies certifiées conformes à tous les Gouvernements signataires et adhérents ainsi qu'au Directeur du Bureau International de Berne pour la Protection de la Propriété Industrielle.

(c) jede gemäß Artikel 11 eingegangene Mitteilung.

ARTIKEL 11

1. Diese Übereinkunft bleibt zeitlich unbegrenzt in Kraft.

2. Jeder Vertragsstaat kann für seinen Bereich diese Übereinkunft dem Generalsekretär des Europarats gegenüber mit einjähriger Frist kündigen.

Zu Urkund dessen haben die hierzu in gehöriger Form ermächtigten Unterzeichneten diese Übereinkunft unterzeichnet.

Geschehen zu Paris, am 11. Dezember 1953 in französischer und englischer Sprache, wobei beide Fassungen gleichermaßen authentisch sind, in einem einzigen Exemplar, das im Archiv des Europarats zu hinterlegen ist. Der Generalsekretär hat beglaubigte Ausfertigungen allen unterzeichnenden und beitretenden Regierungen sowie dem Direktor des Internationalen Büros zum Schutze des gewerblichen Eigentums in Bern zu übermitteln.

ANNEX I

APPLICATION FOR PATENT

I/We the undersigned (1) ....

acting { in my/our own name ....
on behalf of (2) ....

hereby make application for a patent for the invention described in the accompanying specification (and drawings) and entitled ....

I/We the applicant {
claim(s) to be the true (and first) inventor(s) of the invention
claim(s) the following of us (them), namely
to be the true and first inventor(s)
believe(s) .... to be the true and first inventor(s)
claim(s) to be the { Assignee(s) / Personal Representative(s) } of the inventor
by virtue of (3) ....

I/We request that the patent may be granted as a (4) ....

....

....

to Patent (5) { No. ....
Application No. .... dated ....

(6) ....

....

Dated this .... day of .... 19..,

List of documents accompanying this application:

....

....

N.-B. — Delete where not applicable or required.

INSTRUCTIONS

(1) Give the following particulars:
(a) When this form is signed by the applicant(s), here insert his/their first names, surname(s), full address(es) and nationality(ies), or the name and full address where the applicant is not a physical person;
(b) When the form is signed by a nominee of the applicant(s) here insert the first names, surname and full address of the nominee. Note: Nominees cannot apply in certain countries.

(2) In the case (1) (b), insert here the particulars at (1) (a).

(3) Here insert particulars of the assignment or other document.

(4) Here indicate the nature of the protection applied for, e. g. independent patent, patent of importation, patent for an improvement, patent or certificate of addition.

(5) In the case of a divisional application or where otherwise applicable, insert here the number of the related patent, or, where the related patent application is still pending, the number and date of such application.

(6) Insert here, where necessary, any other relevant particulars such as the authorisation of an agent in the country in which the application is made, or, if no such agent is appointed, an address for service in that country.

ANNEXE I

REQUÊTE EN OBTENTION DE BREVET

Le (Les) soussigné(s) (1)..

agissant { en son (leur) nom ....
au nom de (2) .... }

sollicite(nt) par la présente un brevet pour une invention qui fait l'objet de la description (et des dessins) ci-joint et intitulée..

Le (Les) demandeur(s) {
déclare(nt) être le(s) véritable(s) et premier(s) auteur(s) de l'invention
déclare(nt) que parmi eux ....
est (sont) le(s) véritable(s) et premier(s) inventeur(s).
croit(ent) que .... est (sont) le(s) véritable(s) et premier(s) inventeur(s).
déclare(nt) être { l' (les) ayant cause / le(s) représentant(s) / personnel(s) } de l'inventeur
en vertu de (3)...
}

.... demande(nt) que le brevet soit délivré au titre de (4) ....

....

au brevet (5) { No. ....
sollicité par requête n° .... en date .... }

(6) ....

....

Le .... 19..

A ces diverses fins, il (ils) annexe(nt) à la présente les pièces suivantes :

....

....

N.-B. — Biffer les mentions inutiles.

INSTRUCTIONS

(1) Inscrire les indications suivantes :
   (a) si la requête est introduite sans l'intervention d'un mandataire, nom, prénoms, nationalité et adresse complète (personne physique), nom social et siège social (personne morale) ;
   (b) si la requête est introduite par un mandataire, nom, prénoms et adresse complète. Note : Les mandataires ne peuvent introduire une requête dans certains pays.

(2) Dans le cas prévu sub. 1-b, inscrire les indications demandées sub. 1-a.

(3) Inscrire, s'il y a lieu, les indications relatives à l'acte de cession ou de transmission.

(4) Espèce du titre sollicité (brevet principal, brevet d'importation, brevet de perfectionnement, brevet additionnel ou certificat d'addition).

(5) S'il y a lieu, par exemple, dans le cas d'une demande divisionnaire, numéro du brevet de référence, ou, si celui-ci n'est pas encore délivré, numéro et date de la demande.

(6) Inscrire, s'il y a lieu, les autres indications exigées, telles que celles relatives à la désignation d'un mandataire dans le pays où la requête est déposée, ou, s'il n'y a pas de mandataire, l'indication d'une adresse de service dans ce pays.

ANLAGE I

ANTRAG AUF ERTEILUNG EINES PATENTS

Der (Die) Unterzeichnete(n) (1) ....

im eigenen Namen ....) handelnd
im Namen von (2) ....

beantragt (beantragen) hiermit ein Patent für eine Erfindung, die in der beigefügten Beschreibung (und in den beigefügten Zeichnungen) beschrieben und als .... bezeichnet ist.

Der (Die) Antragsteller
- erklärt (erklären), der (die) wirkliche(n) und erste(n) Erfinder zu sein;
- erklärt (erklären), daß unter ihnen .... der (die) wirkliche(n) und erste(n) Erfinder ist (sind);
- glaubt (glauben), daß .... der (die) wirkliche(n) und erste(n) Erfinder ist (sind);
- erklärt (erklären), { der (die) Rechtsnachfolger / der (die) persönliche(n) Vertreter } des Erfinders auf Grund des (der) (3) .... zu sein.

Er (Sie) beantragt (beantragen) die Erteilung des Patents als (4) ....

....

....

zum Patent { Nr. .... / das mit Antrag Nr. .... vom ....

beantragt wurde.

(6) ....

(Datum) .... 19..

Diesem Antrag liegen folgende Unterlagen bei: ....

....

....

N. B. — Nichtzutreffendes ist zu streichen.

ERLÄUTERUNGEN

(1) Es ist anzugeben:
 (a) wenn der Antrag ohne Einschaltung eines Bevollmächtigten eingereicht wird: Name, Vornamen, Staatsangehörigkeit und vollständige Anschrift (bei natürlichen Personen), Firma und Sitz (bei juristischen Personen);
 (b) wenn der Antrag durch einen Bevollmächtigten gestellt wird: Name, Vornamen und vollständige Anschrift.
 Anmerkung: In einigen Ländern können Bevollmächtigte keinen Antrag stellen.

(2) Im Falle (1) (b) sind die unter (1) (a) geforderten Angaben einzusetzen.

(3) Gegebenenfalls sind die Angaben über das Abtretungs- oder Übertragungsgeschäft einzusetzen.

(4) Art des gewünschten Schutzes (Hauptpatent, Einführungspatent, Verbesserungspatent, Zusatzpatent oder Zusatzbescheinigung).

(5) Gegebenenfalls — beispielsweise bei einer ausgeschiedenen Anmeldung — ist die Nummer des Bezugspatents oder, wenn dieses noch nicht erteilt ist, die Nummer und das Datum seiner Anmeldung einzusetzen.

(6) Gegebenenfalls sind sonstige erforderliche Angaben, z. B. hinsichtlich der Bestellung eines Bevollmächtigten in dem Lande, in dem der Antrag gestellt wird, oder, bei Fehlen eines Bevollmächtigten, die Angabe einer Zustellungsanschrift in dem betreffenden Lande einzusetzen.

ANNEX II

CONVENTION APPLICATION FOR PATENT

I/We the undersigned (1) ....

acting {in my/our own name .... / on behalf of (2) ....}

Hereby declare that (an) application(s) for protection for an invention or inventions has(ve) been made in the following country(ies) on the following date(s), namely: —

in .... on ....

by ....

in .... on ....

by ....

in .... on ....

by ....

and that the said application or each of the said applications was the first application in a Convention country.

I am/We are the assignee(s) of the said ....

or the personal representative(s) of the said ....

by virtue of (3) ....

I/We request that a patent may be granted with priority founded on the abovementioned application(s) in a Convention country(ies) for the invention described in the accompanying specification (and drawings) and entitled ....

....

I/We request that the patent may be granted as a (4) ....

....

to Patent (5) {No. .... / Appn. No. .... dated ....}

(6) ....

....

Dated this .... day of ...., 19..

List of documents accompanying this application:

....

....

N.-B. — Delete where not applicable or required.

INSTRUCTIONS

(1) Give the following particulars:

(a) When this form is signed by the applicant(s), here insert his/their first names, surname(s), full address(es) and nationality(ies), or the name and full address where the applicant is not a physical person;

(b) When the form is signed by a nominee of the applicant(s) here insert the first names, surname and full address of the nominee. Note: Nominees cannot apply in certain countries.

(2) In the case (1) (b), insert here the particulars at (1) (a).

(3) Here insert particulars of the assignment or other document.

(4) Here indicate the nature of the protection applied for, e. g. independent patent, patent of importation, patent for an improvement, patent or certificate of addition.

(5) In the case of a divisional application or where otherwise applicable, insert here the number of the related patent, or, where the related patent application is still pending, the number and date of such application.

(6) Insert here, where necessary, any other relevant particulars such as the authorisation of an agent in the country in which the application is made, or, if no such agent is appointed, an address for service in that country.

ANNEXE II

REQUÊTE EN OBTENTION DE BREVET AVEC PRIORITÉ

Le (Les) soussigné(s) (1)..

agissant { en son (leur) nom ....
au nom de (2) ....

déclare(nt) par la présente qu'une (que des) demande(s) de brevet pour une (des) invention(s) a (ont) été déposée(s) dans le (les) pays et à la (aux) date(s) indiquée(s) ci-après :

à .... le ....

par ....

à .... le ....

par ....

à .... le ....

par ....

et que cette (chacune de ces) demande(s) était la première déposée dans un pays adhérant à la Convention.

.... déclare(nt) être l' (les) ayant-cause de ....

.... le(s) représentant(s) personnel(s) de ....

....

en vertu de (3) ....

...... demande(nt) qu'un brevet soit délivré avec priorité à la date de la (des) demande(s) sus-indiquée(s) déposée(s) dans un (des) pays adhérant(s) à la Convention, pour l'invention faisant l'objet de la description (et des dessins) ci-joint et intitulée ....

...... demande(nt) que le brevet soit délivré au titre de (4) ....

....

au brevet (5) { N° ....
requête n° .... en date ....

(6) ....

....

Le .... 19..

Liste des pièces annexées à la présente requête :

....

....

N.-B. — Biffer les mentions inutiles.

INSTRUCTIONS

(1) Inscrire les indications suivantes :
  (a) si la requête est introduite sans l'intervention d'un mandataire, nom, prénoms, nationalité et adresse complète (personne physique), nom social et siège social (personne morale) ;
  (b) si la requête est introduite par un mandataire, nom, prénoms et adresse complète. Note : Les mandataires ne peuvent introduire une requête dans certains pays.

(2) Dans le cas prévu sub. 1-b, inscrire les indications demandées sub. 1-a.

(3) Inscrire, s'il y a lieu, les indications relatives à l'acte de cession ou de transmission.

(4) Espèce du titre sollicité (brevet principal, brevet d'importation, brevet de perfectionnement, brevet additionnel ou certificat d'addition, etc.).

(5) S'il y a lieu, par exemple, dans le cas d'une demande divisionnaire, numéro du brevet de référence, ou, si celui-ci n'est pas encore délivré, numéro et date de la demande.

(6) Inscrire, s'il y a lieu, les autres indications exigées, telles que celles relatives à la désignation d'un mandataire dans le pays où la requête est déposée, ou, s'il n'y a pas de mandataire, l'indication d'une adresse de service dans ce pays.

ANLAGE II

ANTRAG AUF ERTEILUNG EINES PATENTS MIT PRIORITÄT

Der (Die) Unterzeichnete(n) (1) ....

im eigenen Namen .... }
im Namen von (2) .... } handelnd,

erklärt (erklären) hiermit, daß (eine) Patentanmeldung(en) für (eine) Erfindung(en) in dem (den) nachstehenden Land (Ländern) unter dem (den) folgenden Datum (Daten) erfolgt ist (sind):

in .... am ....

durch ....

in .... am ....

durch ....

in .... am ....

durch ....

und daß diese Anmeldung (jede dieser Anmeldungen) die Erstanmeldung in einem der Übereinkunft beigetretenen Lande darstellte.

Er (Sie) erklärt (erklären), der (die) Rechtsnachfolger des ....

der (die) persönliche(n) Vertreter des ....

auf Grund des (der) (3) .... zu sein.

Er (Sie) beantragt (beantragen) für die in der anliegenden Beschreibung (und den beigefügten Zeichnungen) dargestellte Erfindung mit der Bezeichnung ....
die Erteilung eines Patents mit dem Zeitrang des (der) obenerwähnten in (einem) der Übereinkunft beigetretenen Lande (Länder) eingereichten Antrags (Anträge).

Er (Sie) beantragt (beantragen) die Erteilung des Patents als (4) ....

Nr. ....

zum Patent (5) { das mit Antrag Nr. ....
{ vom .... beantragt wurde.

(6) ....

(Datum) .... 19..

Diesem Antrag liegen folgende Unterlagen bei: ....

....

N. B. — Nichtzutreffendes ist zu streichen.

ERLÄUTERUNGEN

(1) Es ist anzugeben:

(a) wenn der Antrag ohne Einschaltung eines Bevollmächtigten eingereicht wird: Name, Vornamen, Staatsangehörigkeit und vollständige Anschrift (bei natürlichen Personen), Firma und Sitz (bei juristischen Personen);

(b) wenn der Antrag durch einen Bevollmächtigten gestellt wird: Name, Vornamen und vollständige Anschrift.
Anmerkung: In einigen Ländern können Bevollmächtigte keinen Antrag stellen.

(2) Im Falle (1) (b) sind die unter (1) (a) geforderten Angaben einzusetzen.

(3) Gegebenenfalls sind die Angaben über das Abtretungs- oder Übertragungsgeschäft einzusetzen.

(4) Art des gewünschten Schutzes (Hauptpatent, Einführungspatent, Verbesserungspatent, Zusatzpatent oder Zusatzbescheinigung usw.).

(5) Gegebenenfalls — beispielsweise bei einer ausgeschiedenen Anmeldung — ist die Nummer des Bezugspatents oder, wenn dieses noch nicht erteilt ist, die Nummer und das Datum seiner Anmeldung einzusetzen.

(6) Gegebenenfalls sind sonstige erforderliche Angaben, z. B. hinsichtlich der Bestellung eines Bevollmächtigten in dem Lande, in dem der Antrag gestellt wird, oder, bei Fehlen eines Bevollmächtigten, die Angabe einer Zustellungsanschrift in dem betreffenden Lande einzusetzen.

für ratifiziert und verspricht im Namen der Republik Österreich die gewissenhafte Erfüllung der darin enthaltenen Bestimmungen.

Zu Urkund dessen ist die vorliegende Ratifikationsurkunde vom Bundespräsidenten unterzeichnet, vom Bundeskanzler, vom Bundesminister für Handel, Gewerbe und Industrie und vom Bundesminister für Auswärtige Angelegenheiten gegengezeichnet und mit dem Staatssiegel der Republik Österreich versehen worden.

Geschehen zu Wien, am 19. Feber 1971

Der Bundespräsident:

Jonas

Der Bundeskanzler:

Kreisky

Der Bundesminister für Handel, Gewerbe und Industrie:

Staribacher

Der Bundesminister für Auswärtige Angelegenheiten:

Kirchschläger

Die österreichische Ratifikationsurkunde ist am 3. März 1971 beim Generalsekretär des Europarates hinterlegt worden. Die vorliegende Übereinkunft tritt somit gemäß ihrem Art. 8 Abs. 3 für Österreich am 1. April 1971 in Kraft.

Derzeit gehören der Übereinkunft folgende Staaten an: Belgien, Bundesrepublik Deutschland, Dänemark, Frankreich, Griechenland, Irland, Island, Israel, Italien, Luxemburg, Niederlande (einschließlich Surinam, Niederländisch West-Indien und Niederländisch-Guinea), Norwegen, Spanien, Schweden, Schweiz, Südafrika, Türkei und das Vereinigte Königreich von Großbritannien und Nordirland (einschließlich der Insel Man).

Kreisky

TREATY
of
COMMERCE AND NAVIGATION BETWEEN JAPAN AND GREAT BRITAIN

Signed at London, 16th day of the 7th month, 27th year of Meiji. Ratifications exchanged at Tokio, 25th day of the 8th month, 27th year of Meiji.

HIS Majesty the Emperor of Japan, and Her Majesty the Queen of the United Kingdom of Great Britain and Ireland, Empress of India, being equally desirous of maintaining the relations of good understanding which happily exist between them, by extending and increasing the intercourse between their respective States, and being convinced that this object cannot better be accomplished than by revising the Treaties hitherto existing between the two countries, have resolved to complete such a revision, based upon principles of equity and mutual benefit, and, for that purpose, have named as their Plenipotentiaries, that is to say:

His Majesty the Emperor of Japan, Viscount Aoki Siuzo, Junii, first class of the Imperial Order of the Sacred Treasure, His Majesty's Envoy Extraordinary and Minister Plenipotentiary at the Court of St. James';

And Her Majesty the Queen of the United Kingdom of Great Britain and Ireland, Empress of India, the Right Honourable John, Earl of Kimberley, Knight of the Most Noble Order of the Garter, &c., &c., Her Britannic Majesty's Secretary of State for Foreign Affairs;

Who, after having communicated to each other their Full Powers, found to be in good and due form, have agreed upon and concluded the following Articles:—

Article I

The subjects of each of the two High Contracting Parties shall have full liberty to enter, travel, or reside in any part of the dominions and possessions of the other Contracting Party, and shall enjoy full and perfect protection for their persons and property.

They shall have free and easy access to the Courts of Justice in pursuit and defence of their rights; they shall be at liberty equally with native subjects to choose and employ lawyers, advocates, and representatives to pursue and defend their rights before such Courts, and in all other matters connected with the administration of justice they shall enjoy all the rights and privileges enjoyed by native subjects.

In whatever relates to rights of residence and travel; to the possession of goods and effects of any kind; to the succession to personal estate, by will or otherwise, and the disposal of property of any sort in any manner whatsoever which they may lawfully acquire, the subjects of each Contracting Party shall enjoy in the dominions and possessions of the other the same privileges, liberties, and rights, and shall be subject to no higher imposts or charges in these respects than native subjects or citizens of the most favoured nation. The subjects of each of the Contracting Parties shall enjoy in the dominions and possessions of the other entire liberty of conscience, and, subject to the Laws, Ordinances, and Regulations, shall enjoy the right of private or public exercise of their worship, and also the right of burying their respective countrymen, according to their religious customs, in such suitable and convenient places as may be established and maintained for that purpose.

They shall not be compelled, under any pretext whatsoever, to pay any charges or taxes other or higher than those that are, or may be, paid by native subjects, or subjects or citizens of the most favoured nation.

Article II

The subjects of either of the Contracting Parties residing in the dominions and possessions of the other shall be exempted from all compulsory military service whatsoever, whether in the army, navy, National Guard, or militia; from all contributions imposed in lieu of personal service; and from all forced loans or military exactions or contributions.

Article III

There shall be reciprocal freedom of commerce and navigation between the dominions and possessions of the two High Contracting Parties.

The subjects of each of the High Contracting Parties may trade in any part of the dominions and possessions of the other by wholesale or retail in all kinds of produce, manufactures, and merchandize of lawful commerce, either in person or by agents, singly, or in partnerships with foreigners or native subjects; and they may there own or hire and occupy the houses, manufactories, warehouses, shops, and premises which may be necessary for them, and lease land for residential and commercial purposes, conforming themselves to the Laws, Police, and Customs Regulations of the country like native subjects.

They shall have liberty to come with their ships and cargoes to all places, ports, and rivers in the dominions and possessions of the other which are or may be opened to foreign commerce, and shall enjoy, respectively, the same treatment in matters of commerce and navigation as native subjects, or subjects or citizens of the most favoured nation, without having to pay taxes, imposts, or duties, of whatever nature or under whatever denomination levied in the name or for the profit of the Government, public functionaries, private individuals, Corporations, or establishments of any kind, other or greater than those paid by native subjects, or subjects or citizens of the most favoured nation, subject always to the Laws, Ordinances, and Regulations of each country.

Article IV

The dwellings, manufactories, warehouses, and shops of the subjects of each of the High Contracting Parties in the dominions and possessions of the other, and all premises appertaining thereto destined for purposes of residence or commerce, shall be respected.

It shall not be allowable to proceed to make a search of, or a domiciliary visit to, such dwellings and premises, or to examine or inspect books, papers, or accounts, except under the conditions and with the forms prescribed by the Laws, Ordinances, and Regulations for subjects of the country.

Article V

No other or higher duties shall be imposed on the importation into the dominions and possessions of Her Britannic Majesty of any article, the produce or manufacture of the dominions and possessions of His Majesty the Emperor of Japan, from whatever place arriving; and no other or higher duties shall be imposed on the importation into the dominions and possessions of His Majesty the Emperor of Japan of any article, the produce or manufacture of the dominions and possessions of Her Britannic Majesty, from whatever place arriving, than on the like article produced or manufactured in any other foreign country; nor shall any prohibition be maintained or imposed on the importation of any article, the produce or manufacture of the dominions and possessions of either of the High Contracting Parties, into the dominions and possessions of the other, from whatever place arriving, which shall not equally extend to the importation of the like article, being the produce or manufacture of any other country. This last provision is not applicable to the sanitary and other prohibitions occasioned by the necessity of protecting the safety of persons, or of cattle, or of plants useful to agriculture.

Article VI

No other or higher duties or charges shall be imposed in the dominions and possessions of either of the High Contracting Parties on the exportation of any article to the dominions and possessions of the other than such as are, or may be, payable on the exportation of the like article to any other foreign country; nor shall any prohibition be imposed on the exportation of any article from the dominions and possessions of either of the two Contracting Parties to the dominions and possessions of the other which shall not equally extend to the exportation of the like article to any other country.

Article VII

The subjects of each of the High Contracting Parties shall enjoy in the dominions and possessions of the other exemption from all transit duties, and a perfect equality of treatment with native subjects in all that relates to warehousing, bounties, facilities, and drawbacks.

Article VIII

All articles which are or may be legally imported into the ports of the dominions and possessions of His Majesty the Emperor of Japan in Japanese vessels may likewise be imported into those ports in British vessels, without being liable to any other or higher duties or charges of whatever denomination than if such articles were imported in Japanese vessels; and reciprocally, all articles which are or may be legally imported into the ports of the dominions and possessions of Her Britannic Majesty in British vessels may likewise be imported into those ports in Japanese vessels, without being liable to any other or higher duties or charges of whatever denomination than if such articles were imported in British vessels. Such reciprocal equality of treatment shall take effect without distinction, whether such articles come directly from the place of origin or from any other place.

In the same manner there shall be perfect equality of treatment in regard to exportation, so that the same export duties shall be paid and the same bounties and drawbacks allowed in the dominions and possessions of either of the High Contracting Parties on the exportation of any article which is or may be legally exported therefrom, whether such exportation shall take place in Japanese or in British vessels, and whatever may be the place of destination, whether a port of either of the Contracting Parties or of any third Power.

Article IX

No duties of tonnage, harbour, pilotage, lighthouse, quarantine, or other similar or corresponding duties of whatever nature or under whatever denomination, levied in the name or for the profit of the Government, public functionaries, private individuals, Corporations, or establishments of any kind, shall be imposed in the ports of the dominions and possessions of either country upon the vessels of the other country which shall not equally and under the same conditions be imposed in the like cases on national vessels in general or vessels of the most favoured nation. Such equality of treatment shall apply reciprocally to the respective vessels, from whatever port or place they may arrive, and whatever may be their place of destination.

Article X

In all that regards the stationing, loading, and unloading of vessels in the ports, basins, docks, roadsteads, harbours, or rivers of the dominions and possessions of the two countries, no privilege shall be granted to national vessels which shall not be equally granted to vessels of the other country; and the intention of the High Contracting Parties being that in this respect also the respective vessels shall be treated on the footing of perfect equality.

Article XI

The coasting trade of both the High Contracting Parties is excepted from the provisions of the present Treaty, and shall be regulated according to the Laws, Ordinances, and Regulations of Japan and of Great Britain respectively. It is, however, understood that Japanese subjects in the dominions and possessions of Her Britannic Majesty, and British subjects in the dominions and possessions of His Majesty the Emperor of Japan, shall enjoy in this respect the rights which are or may be granted under such Laws, Ordinances, and Regulations to the subjects or citizens of any other country.

A Japanese vessel laden in a foreign country with cargo destined for two or more ports in the dominions and possessions of Her Britannic Majesty, and a British vessel laden in a foreign country with cargo destined for two or more ports in the dominions and possessions of His Majesty the Emperor of Japan, may discharge a portion of her cargo at one port, and continue her voyage to the other port or ports of destination where foreign trade is permitted, for the purpose of landing the remainder of her original cargo there, subject always to the Laws and Custom-house Regulations of the two countries.

The Japanese Government, however, agrees to allow British vessels to continue, as heretofore, for the period of the duration of the present Treaty, to carry cargo between the existing open ports of the Empire, excepting to or from the ports of Osaka, Niigata, and Ebisuminato.

Article XII

Any ship of war or merchant-vessel of either of the High Contracting Parties which may be compelled by stress of weather, or by reason of any other distress, to take shelter in a port of the other, shall be at liberty to refit therein, to procure all necessary supplies, and to put to sea again, without paying any dues other than such as would be payable by national vessels. In case, however, the master of a merchant-vessel should be under the necessity of disposing of a part of his cargo in order to defray the expenses, he shall be bound to conform to the Regulations and Tariffs of the place to which he may have come.

If any ship of war or merchant-vessel of one of the Contracting Parties should run aground or be wrecked upon the coasts of the other, the local authorities shall inform the Consul-General, Consul, Vice-Consul, or Consular Agent of the district of the occurrence, or if there be no such Consular officer, they shall inform the Consul-General, Consul, Vice-Consul, or Consular Agent of the nearest district.

All proceedings relative to the salvage of Japanese vessels

wrecked or cast on shore in the territorial waters of Her Britannic Majesty shall take place in accordance with the Laws, Ordinances, and Regulations of Great Britain, and reciprocally, all measures of salvage relative to British vessels wrecked or cast on shore in the territorial waters of His Majesty the Emperor of Japan shall take place in accordance with the Laws, Ordinances, and Regulations of Japan.

Such stranded or wrecked ship or vessel, and all parts thereof, and all furnitures and appurtenances belonging therunto, and all goods and merchandize saved therefrom, including those which may have been cast into the sea, or the proceeds thereof, if sold, as well as all papers found on board such stranded or wrecked ship or vessel, shall be given up to the owners or their agents, when claimed by them. If such owners or agents are not on the spot, the same shall be delivered to the respective Consuls-General, Consuls, Vice-Consuls, or Consular Agents upon being claimed by them within the period fixed by the laws of the country and such Consular officers, owners, or agents shall pay only the expenses incurred in the preservation of the property, together with the salvage or other expenses which would have been payable in the case of a wreck of a national vessel.

The goods and merchandize saved from the wreck shall be exempt from all the duties of the Customs unless cleared for consumption, in which case they shall pay the ordinary duties.

When a ship or vessel belonging to the subjects of one of the Contracting Parties is stranded or wrecked in the territories of the other, the respective Consuls-General, Consuls, Vice-Consuls, and Consular Agents shall be authorized, in case the owner or master, or other agent of the owner, is not present, to lend their official assistance in order to afford the necessary assistance to the subjects of the respective States. The same rule shall apply in case the owner, master, or other agent is present, but requires such assistance to be given.

Article XIII

All vessels which, according to Japanese law, are to be deemed Japanese vessels, and all vessels which, according to British law, are to be deemed British vessels, shall, for the purposes of this Treaty, be deemed Japanese and British vessels respectively.

Article XIV

The Consuls-General, Consuls, Vice-Consuls, and Consular Agents of each of the Contracting Parties, residing in the dominions and possessions of the other, shall receive from the local authorities such assistance as can by law be given to them for the recovery of deserters from the vessels of their respective countries.

It is understood that this stipulation shall not apply to the subjects of the country where the desertion takes place.

Article XV

The High Contracting Parties agree that, in all that concerns commerce and navigation, any privilege, favour, or immunity which either Contracting Party has actually granted, or may hereafter grant, to the Government, ships, subjects, or citizens of any other State, shall be extended immediately and unconditionally to the Government, ships, subjects, or citizens of the other Contracting Party, it being their intention that the trade and navigation of each country shall be placed, in all respects, by the other on the footing of the most favoured nation.

Article XVI

Each of the High Contracting Parties may appoint Consuls-General, Consuls, Vice-Consuls, Pro-Consuls, and Consular Agents in all the ports, cities, and places of the other, except in those where it may not be convenient to recognize such officers.

This exception, however, shall not be made in regard to one of the Contracting Parties without being made likewise in regard to every other Power.

The Consuls-General, Consuls, Vice-Consuls, Pro-Consuls, and Consular Agents may exercise all functions, and shall enjoy all privileges, exemptions, and immunities which are, or may hereafter be, granted to Consular officers of the most favoured nation.

Article XVII

The subjects of each of the High Contracting Parties shall enjoy in the dominions and possessions of the other the same protection as native subjects in regard to patents, trademarks, and designs, upon fulfillment of the formalities prescribed by law.

Article XVIII

Her Britannic Majesty's Government, so far as they are concerned, give their consent to the following arrangement:—

The several foreign Settlements in Japan shall be incorporated with the respective Japanese Communes, and shall thenceforth form part of the general municipal system of Japan.

The competent Japanese authorities shall thereupon assume all municipal obligations and duties in respect thereof, and the common funds and property, if any, belonging to such Settlements, shall at the same time be transferred to the said Japanese authorities.

When such incorporation takes place existing leases in perpetuity under which property is now held in the said Settlements shall be confirmed, and no conditions whatsoever other than those contained in such existing leases shall be imposed in respect of such property. It is, however, understood that the Consular authorities mentioned in the same are in all cases to be replaced by the Japanese authorities.

All lands which may previously have been granted by the Japanese Government free of rent for the public purposes of the said Settlements subject to the right of eminent domain shall be permanently reserved free of all taxes and charges for the public purposes for which they were originally set apart.

Article XIX

The stipulations of the present Treaty shall be applicable, so far as the laws permit, to all the Colonies and foreign possessions of Her Britannic Majesty, excepting to those hereinafter named, that is to say, except to—

India.
The Dominion of Canada.
Newfoundland.
The Cape.
Natal.
New South Wales.
Victoria.
Queensland.
Tasmania.
South Australia.
Western Australia.
New Zealand.

Provided always that the stipulations of the present Treaty shall be made applicable to any of the above-named Colonies or foreign possessions on whose behalf notice to that effect shall have been given to the Japanese Government by Her Britannic Majesty's Representative at Tokio within two years from the date of the exchange of ratifications of the present Treaty.

Article XX

The present Treaty shall, from the date it comes into force, be substituted in place of the Conventions respectively of the 23rd day of the 8th month of the 7th year of Kayei, corresponding to the 14th day of October, 1854, and of the 13th day of the 5th month of the 2nd year of Keiou, corresponding to the 25th day of June, 1866, the Treaty of the 18th day of the 7th month of the 5th year of Ansei, corresponding to the 26th day of August, 1858, and all Arrangements and Agreements subsidiary thereto concluded or existing between the High Contracting Parties; and from the same date such Conventions, Treaty, Arrangements, and Agreements shall cease to be binding, and, in consequence, the jurisdiction then exercised by British Courts in Japan, and all the exceptional privilege, exemptions, and immunities then enjoyed by British subjects as a part of or appurtenant to such jurisdiction, shall absolutely and without notice cease and determine, and thereafter all such jurisdiction shall be assumed and exercised by Japanese Courts.

Article XXI

The present Treaty shall not take effect until at least five years after its signature. It shall come into force one year after His Imperial Japanese Majesty's Government shall have given notice to Her Britannic Majesty's Government of its wish to have the same brought into operation. Such notice may be given at any time after the expiration of four years from the date hereof. The Treaty shall remain in force for the period of twelve years from the date it goes into operation.

Either High Contracting Party shall have the right, at any time after eleven years shall have elapsed from the date this Treaty takes effect, to give notice to the other of its intention to terminate the same, and at the expiration of twelve months after such notice is given this Treaty shall wholly cease and determine.

Article XXII

The present Treaty shall be ratified, and the ratifications thereof shall be exchanged at Tokio as soon as possible, and not later than six months from the present date.

In witness whereof the respective Plenipotentiaries have signed the same and have affixed thereto the seal of their arms.

Done at London, in duplicate, this sixteenth day of the seventh month of the twenty-seventh year of Meiji.

(L. S.) AOKI.
(L. S.) KIMBERLEY.

Protocol

THE Government of His Majesty the Emperor of Japan and the Government of Her Majesty the Queen of Great Britain and Ireland and Empress of India, deeming it advisable in the interests of both countries to regulate certain special matters of mutual concern, apart from the Treaty of Commerce and Navigation signed this day, have, through their respective Plenipotentiaries, agreed upon the following stipulations—

1. It is agreed by the Contracting Parties that one month after the exchange of the ratifications of the Treaty of Commerce and Navigation signed this day, the Import Tariff hereunto annexed shall, subject to the provisions of Article XXIII of the Treaty of 1858 at present subsisting between the Contracting Parties, as long as the said Treaty remains in force and thereafter, subject to the provisions of Articles V and XV of the Treaty signed this day, be applicable to the articles therein enumerated, being the growth, produce, or manufacture of the dominions and possessions of Her Britannic Majesty, upon importation into Japan. But nothing contained in this Protocol, or the Tariff hereunto annexed, shall be held to limit or qualify the right of the Japanese Government to restrict or to prohibit the importation of adulterated drugs, medicines, food, or beverages; indecent or obscene prints, paintings, books, cards, lithographic or other engravings, photographs, or any other indecent or obscene articles; articles in violation of patent, trademark, or copyright laws of Japan; or any other article which for sanitary reasons, or in view of public security or morals, might offer any danger.

The *ad valorem* duties established by the said Tariff shall, so far as may be deemed practicable, be converted into specific duties by a Supplementary Convention, which shall be concluded between the two Governments within six months from the date of this Protocol; the medium prices, as shown by the Japanese Customs Returns during the six calendar months preceding the date of the present Protocol, with the addition of the cost of insurance and transportation from the place of purchase, production, or fabrication, to the port of discharge, as well as commission, if any, shall be taken as the basis for such conversion. In the event of the Supplementary Convention not having come into force before the expiration of the period fixed for the said Tariff to take effect, *ad valorem* duties in conformity with the rule recited at the end of the said Tariff shall, in the meantime, be levied.

In respect of articles not enumerated in the said Tariff, the General Statutory Tariff of Japan for the time being in force shall, from the same time, apply, subject, as aforesaid, to the provisions of Article XXIII of the Treaty of 1858 and Articles V and XV of the Treaty signed this day respectively.

From the date the Tariffs aforesaid take effect, the Import Tariff now in operation in Japan in respect of goods and merchandize imported into Japan by British subjects shall cease to be binding.

In all other respects the stipulations of the existing Treaties and Conventions shall be maintained unconditionally until the time when the Treaty of Commerce and Navigation signed this day comes into force.

2. The Japanese Government, pending the opening of the country to British subjects, agrees to extend the existing passport system in such a manner as to allow British subjects, on the production of a certificate of recommendation from the British Representative in Tokio, or from any of Her Majesty's Consuls at the open ports in Japan, to obtain upon application passports available for any part of the country, and for any period not exceeding twelve months, from the Imperial Japanese Foreign Office in Tokio, or from the chief authorities in the Prefecture in which an open port is situated; it being understood that the existing Rules and Regulations governing British subjects who visit the interior of the Empire are to be maintained.

3. The Japanese Government undertakes, before the cessation of British Consular jurisdiction in Japan, to join the International Conventions for the Protection of Industrial Property and Copyright.

4. It is understood between the two High Contracting Parties that, if Japan thinks it necessary at any time to levy an additional duty on the production or manufacture of refined sugar in Japan, an increased customs duty equivalent in amount may be levied on British refined sugar when imported into Japan, so long as such additional excise tax or inland duty continues to be raised.

Provided always that British refined sugar shall in this respect be entitled to the treatment accorded to refined sugar being the produce or manufacture of the most favoured nation.

5. The undersigned Plenipotentiaries have agreed that this Protocol shall be submitted to the two High Contracting Parties at the

same time as the Treaty of Commerce and Navigation signed this day, and that when the said Treaty is ratified the agreements contained in the Protocol shall also equally be considered as approved, without the necessity of a further formal ratification.

It is agreed that this Protocol shall terminate at the same time the said Treaty ceases to be binding.

In witness whereof the respective Plenipotentiaries have signed the same, and have affixed thereto the seal of their arms.

Done at London, in duplicate, this sixteenth day of the seventh month of the twenty-seventh year of Meiji.

(L. S.) AOKI.
(L. S.) KIMBERLEY.

INDEX

Index